UNDERSTANDING PRAGMATIC MARKERS
MARKERS
A Variational Pragmatic Approach

Karin Aijmer

EDINBURGH
University Press

© Karin Aijmer, 2013

Edinburgh University Press Ltd
22 George Square, Edinburgh EH8 9LF

www.euppublishing.com

Typeset in 10/12 Ehrhardt
by Servis Filmsetting Ltd, Stockport, Cheshire, and
printed and bound in Great Britain by
CPI Group (UK) Ltd, Croydon CR0 4YY

A CIP record for this book is available from the British Library

ISBN 978 0 7486 3549 8 (hardback)
ISBN 978 0 7486 3550 4 (paperback)
ISBN 978 0 7486 3551 1 (webready PDF)
ISBN 978 0 7486 8165 5 (epub)
ISBN 978 0 7486 8164 8 (Amazon ebook)

The right of Karin Aijmer
to be identified as author of this work
has been asserted in accordance with
the Copyright, Designs and Patents Act 1988.

Contents

Acknowledgements

I am deeply grateful to many people who have read different chapters of the book and provided valuable comments. I especially want to thank Bengt Altenberg, Gisle Andersen, Ad Foolen, Jennifer Herriman, Joybrato Mukherjee and his students, Heike Pichler and Anna-Brita Stenström.

Symbols used in Discourse Transcriptions

<,>	short pause
..	short pause
<,,>	long pause
. . .	long pause
=	lengthening
<.> . . . </.>	incomplete words
<O> . . . </O>	untranscribed text
[ ]	speech overlap
<X . . . X>	uncertain hearing
(H)	inhalation
%	glottal stop
(TSK)	type of vocal noise

1

Introduction

Communication processes do not merely apply to society: they are indefinitely varied as to form and meaning for the various types of personal relationships into which society resolves itself. Thus a fixed type of conduct or a linguistic symbol has by no means necessarily the same communicative significance within the confines of the family, among the members of an economic group, and in the nation at large. (Sapir [1931] 1951)

1.1 Introduction

A recent edited volume of articles on pragmatic markers describes the study of pragmatic markers as follows:

> There are very many studies of discourse particles on the market, and by now it is almost impossible to find one's way through the jungle of publications. For a newcomer to the field, it is furthermore often very difficult to find the bits and pieces that constitute an original model of the meanings and functions of discourse particles. Moreover, the studies available so far are hardly comparable: the approaches vary with respect to very many different aspects: the language(s) under consideration, the items taken into account, the terminology used, the functions considered, the problems focussed on, and the methodologies employed. (Fischer 2006: 1)

Research on pragmatic markers has avalanched in recent years and pragmatic markers have been promoted to a major area in pragmatics as shown by the large number of approaches devoted to the topic. The approaches are synchronic and diachronic, formal and informal; 'approaches building on text-linguistic models; models of general cognitive processing or interactively relevant domains of discourse; as well as approaches concentrating on syntactic, semantic, pragmatic, or prosodic aspects' (Fischer 2006: 1).

Notwithstanding the recent spate of research on pragmatic markers from different perspectives some challenges remain. The approach in this book is inspired by recent ideas in pragmatics on variation in language use which can be explained by factors such as text type, activity type, speakers, region, degree of formality, etc.

The time now seems ripe for a book on pragmatic markers paying attention to their variation with regard to social, cultural and regional factors. In an earlier study of pragmatic markers, I wrote that 'the sociolinguistic analysis does not have a prominent place' (Aijmer 2002: 213). However, it was pointed out (ibid. 220) that we 'need to bring in sociolinguistic factors such as the type of speaker and, in particular, text type in order to describe how they differ from each other'.

The hypothesis in this book is that in addition to a general analysis of pragmatic markers we need to take into account their occurrence in different varieties (of English), text types and activity types. The aim of this work is accordingly to study some selected pragmatic markers and their distribution across different text types, dialogues or monologues, situations (activity types), varieties of English and across time. However, there are many contextual variables and the present study only presents a modest beginning in the study of pragmatic markers in different contexts.

A major inspiration for studying pragmatic markers in variable contexts is the emergence of a new discipline: 'variational pragmatics' (Barron and Schneider 2009: 426) and new ideas about factors causing variation. Variational pragmatics has the goal of 'examining pragmatic variation across geographical and social varieties of language, and determining the impact of such factors as region, social class, gender, age and ethnicity on communicative language use' (Schneider and Barron 2008: 1). Variational pragmatics can be said to go hand in hand with a critical attitude to classic variational studies of sociolinguistic variables since the methods used in this tradition may be less suitable to study discourse variation. The aim is to go beyond a concern with sociolinguistic categories such as age and gender by introducing a pragmatic level on which language is studied as speech acts or in terms of turn-taking and topic organisation. Thus variational pragmatics highlights both 'the failure of sociolinguistics to address the pragmatic level of language to any systematic extent' and 'the failure of pragmatics to address variation due to macrosocial variables such as region, socio–economic status, ethnic identity, gender and age' (Barron and Schneider 2009: 436).

The majority of studies in variational pragmatics have so far mainly dealt with regional and social differences in the realisation of speech acts. By now we have a number of 'paradigm' studies showing how speech acts such as requests vary across different regional and social varieties. As a result we know quite a lot about the issues, the social factors involved and the methodologies used to study the variation of speech acts. But there is also a need for variational studies of pragmatic markers. Like speech acts, pragmatic markers are used variably depending on the region, the social situation and the identity of the speaker. Expanding the study of pragmatic markers to look at their variation depending on such contextual factors broadens the area of study and can also be expected to result in a better knowledge of pragmatic markers in general.

Pragmatic markers have been studied earlier from a sociolinguistic point of view. However, the focus in earlier studies has been on the influence of sociolinguistic variables such as age, gender and class on the use of pragmatic markers. As a result we have some knowledge about their dependence on the users. For example, in a number of articles Janet Holmes has studied the form and functions of pragmatic markers and their use by men and women in New Zealand English (1986, 1988a, 1988b, 1990) and Andersen

(2001) studied *like* and *innit* in 'youngspeak' linking the sociolinguistic facts to gram-maticalisation. However we can also expect pragmatic markers to be used differently depending on text type and social activity. We may now be watching a change of focus. According to Pichler, 'the usage of discourse-pragmatic features is strongly constrained by the interactional and situational context of their occurrence to the extent even that these factors may outrank the effect of social factors on discourse variability'. Among the 'wide array of factors' which may be assumed to have an effect on variation and change Pichler mentions, for example, discourse type and activity context, topic, purpose of and attitudes to the interaction, speaker roles and relationship and the communicative channel. These features can be reflected in frequencies and in different functions (Pichler 2010: 584).

Another approach is to broaden the study of pragmatic markers to different regional varieties. Pragmatic markers have been shown to be used differently in British and American English although some of the differences are quantitative only (cf. Aijmer 2002). It is also the case that 'new' pragmatic markers (or uses of pragmatic markers) travel quickly to other varieties. *Like* and *be like* (the latter referred to as an innovation in American English) 'are among the fastest-spreading constructions in English today' (Mair 2009: 22). *Be like* is for instance spreading in American English and is reported as an innovation, for example, in Australian and Canadian English (cf. Mair 2009: 22 for references to ongoing research). In this work I will be less concerned with factors such as age, gender and class and focus instead on the importance of text type (used here with reference to both speech and writing), the social situation (chat, dispute, etc.) and the regional variety of English.

We cannot discuss pragmatic markers in different text types and varieties of English without considering 'where we are now' in the area of pragmatic research. Recently much has happened in the discussion of the theoretical framework and the categorisation of the functions of pragmatic markers (cf. Innes 2010: 96; Fischer 2006). However there is little agreement on basic issues such as the definition of pragmatic markers, terminology, and how many meanings they can have. As Pons Bordería (2006: 94) describes the present situation, pragmatic marker research is 'a melting pot of problems and perspectives'. (See Fischer 2006 for an extensive discussion of these larger issues and controversies.)

By studying the formal and functional variability of pragmatic markers in different text types and situations, we can still hope to contribute to the discussion of larger issues such as the influence of contextual variables on the function and meaning of pragmatic markers and whether they have a single meaning. The studies of the individual pragmatic markers are corpus-based and made possible by the existence of spoken corpora which include several varieties. A number of different corpora will be used to examine how their frequencies, form and function vary across different regional varieties, text types, activity types, etc. (see Section 1.3).

The present chapter is a general chapter where I discuss some basic assumptions underlying the empirical case studies. The definition of pragmatic markers in this work is discussed in Section 1.2. Pragmatic markers are described as reflexive or metalinguistic indicators (Section 1.2.1) and as contextualisation cues (Section 1.2.2). Section 1.3 deals with the corpus-linguistic methodology. Section 1.4 discusses the description of the relationship between pragmatic markers and context in some linguistic theories focusing on 'integrative' theories (1.4.1), relevance theory (1.4.2) and especially the theory of meaning potentials (1.4.3). The contextual parameters and the importance of stance are discussed in Section 1.5 and the formal features of pragmatic markers in Section 1.6. The functions of pragmatic markers are dealt with in Section 1.7. Section 1.8 summarises the discussion in this chapter.

The bulk of this book consists of case studies of a few selected pragmatic markers. The pragmatic marker *well* occupies a central position. This is not surprising since it is one of the most frequent markers. It has been studied extensively in earlier work. However these works have focused on 'large' issues such as whether *well* is a pragmatic marker, what 'core' meaning it has, whether it is homonymous or polysemous, etc. Moreover *well* has been studied primarily in conversation. As a result, we know very little about its functions in other contexts although we are beginning to see some work which problematises the fact that *well* is used in new or different ways when we move away from conversation (see also Chapter 2). The pragmatic markers *actually* and *in fact* discussed in Chapter 3 seem to have similar meanings and can sometimes be interchangeable. However, a more detailed study of their usage domains shows that there are both similarities and differences between them and that it is important to consider their uses in different situations and text types. Pragmatic markers such as *and that sort of thing* and *or something* vary both with regard to age, gender and with regard to different dialects as has been shown in earlier work. In Chapter 4 their usage is studied in different national varieties of English.

1.2 Definition of pragmatic markers in this work

The terms contextualisation cue and metalinguistic indicator have been used in sociolinguistic and anthropological work to describe pragmatic markers with reference to their functions in the communication situation and their relation to the context. These terms correspond well to how I understand the general function of a pragmatic marker as will be obvious from the discussion in the following sub-sections. The aim of this and the following sections is to define the role of pragmatic markers within a general pragmatic theory focusing on the language user and the relationship between meaning and context. Pragmatic markers are 'surface phenomena'. On a deeper level they are reflexive i.e. they 'mirror' the speaker's mental processes as envisaged in 'the fabric of talk-in-interaction' commenting on what goes on in the speaker's mind (Redeker 2006).

1.2.1 Pragmatic markers and reflexivity

Reflexivity is manifested as the speaker's awareness of the linguistic choices made both with regard to what to say and how to say it (Verschueren 1999: 187). Speakers have access to their own speech production and closely attend to what is going on; they are 'metalinguistically aware' of what type of interaction they are involved in, if something goes wrong in the process, and what their attitudes are.

The speaker's cognitive processes are hidden to observation. However, pragmatic markers (and other devices) can emerge as overt indicators of (or windows on) ongoing metalinguistic activity in the speaker's mind.

> Speech is permeated by reflexive activity as speakers remark on language, report utterances, index and describe aspects of the speech event. [. . .] This reflexivity

is so pervasive and essential that we can say that language is, by nature, funda-
mentally reflexive. (Lucy 1993:11; also quoted in Aijmer et al. 2006: 106)

Pragmatic markers function as indicators of metapragmatic awareness along with other
features such as prosody, hesitation, pausing: 'a wide range of indicators of metapragmatic
awareness passes under the variable and often overlapping labels discourse markers, discourse particles or pragmatic particles' (Verschueren 1999: 189). This property accounts,
for example, for the ability of pragmatic markers to reflect on and organise the discourse,
for example to make it more coherent on the local and global level. *Well* for instance
'remarks on' the planning going on in the speaker's mind or accompanies processes
such as reformulation or revision. It can be described as a reflexive 'utterance signal'
which can convey conversational 'uptake' (feedback on a preceding utterance) or project
a new utterance. It can also change the context (e.g. signalling a new stage of a social
activity).

Their ability to project a new stage in the discourse (a new activity, speech act, or
text) is an important aspect of metalinguistic indicators. They therefore have a crucial
role in controlling and changing the progress of the discourse. We can distinguish two
ways in which a pragmatic marker (or another indexical sign) can project an element of
the context following Silverstein (1992). Silverstein distinguishes between metalinguistic
indicators which presuppose something about their context-of-occurrence and those
which alter some aspect of the existing linguistic context.

> Any indexical sign can index the context in two ways which have to do
> with the appropriateness of language or its effectiveness: Any indexical sign
> form in occurring . . . hovers between two contractible relationships to its
> 'contextual' surround: the signal form as occurring either PRESUPPOSES
> (hence, indexes) something about its context-of-occurrence, or ENTAILS
> ('CREATES') (and hence indexes) something about its context-of-occurrence,
> these *co-present* dimensions of indexicality being sometimes seen as essential
> properties of the signs themselves, 'appropriateness-to-context-of-occurrence'
> and 'effectiveness-in-context-of-occurrence'. (Silverstein 1992: 36; quoted from
> Haviland 1996: 280)

Presupposing depends upon aspects of the context which exist independent of speech
while creative forms alter it. What is interesting in this connection is that pragmatic
markers have the defining property that they can be creative: they index the context by
altering an existing context and creating a new (linguistic or social) context. What the
new (social) context is depends for example on the activity (the context entailed by the
pragmatic marker is different in a debate and in a classroom lesson). Speakers may thus
use pragmatic markers to update the interlocutor about an upcoming shift to a different
topic, a new stage in the debate or the end of the classroom lesson.

In addition to the function of monitoring the speaker's progression through the discourse 'any indexical sign' can have a rhetorical or dialogical function in the interaction
(cf. Fischer 2000: 283). This is the case when speakers use a pragmatic marker with a
rhetorical function to take up stances either agreeing or disagreeing with what is said and
with the hearer (cf. Section 1.5).

1.2.2 Pragmatic markers as contextualisation cues

Pragmatic markers typically mark off segments in the discourse thus helping the hearer to understand how the stream of talk is organised. However, positioning within the discourse is not sufficient to explain how the propositional content is to be interpreted, in particular if we analyse the uses of pragmatic markers in different text types and situations. According to Gumperz (1996: 379):

> [c]onversational analysts seek to account for the workings of speech exchanges through turn-by-turn examination of their sequential ordering (Schegloff 1986). Yet while interpretation always depends on how acts are positioned within the stream of talk, positioning alone is not enough. Even with relatively simple utterances, propositional content can only be assessed . . ., with reference to shared frames or common ground.

When we examine pragmatic markers in other text types than conversation they can be used in a number of specialised ways which can only be explained with reference to the characteristic features of the text type or the situation where they are found. Pragmatic markers are for example used to signal the transition to a new topic, activity, argument, stage in a narrative, a new speaker in a debate, the drawing-to-a-close of a telephone conversation, etc. Studying pragmatic markers in institutionalised discourse draws attention to the fact that we need to consider a more 'abstract' context than positioning or the immediate linguistic context, namely the interactants' shared knowledge of the speech event.

Such shared knowledge is especially important if the roles of the speakers and the organisation of the discourse are 'fixed' to some extent. In De Fina's (1997) study of Spanish *bien* in the classroom the interpretation is made on the basis of a 'teaching frame' where the teacher has a privileged role and *bien* is inserted in 'slots' marking the transition from one classroom activity to another.

De Fina (1997) described *bien* (English 'well') as a contextualisation cue quoting Gumperz:

> A contextualization cue is one of a cluster of indexical signs . . . produced in the act of speaking that jointly index, that is, invoke, a frame of interpretation for the rest of the linguistic content of the utterance. (Gumperz 1996: 379)

Gumperz restricted himself to cues such as prosody, gestures or shifts (code switches or style shifts) which are generally less salient than pragmatic markers. However, pragmatic markers are equally important as contextualisation cues. They can, for instance, signal a change in the social context (a change of frames or an activity within a frame) and enable hearers to infer the speaker's strategies and intentions on a moment-to-moment basis in the interaction (what is happening now, who is doing what): 'As metapragmatic signs, contextualization cues represent speakers' ways of signaling and providing information to interlocutors and audience about how language is being used at any point in the ongoing stream of talk' (Gumperz 1996: 366).

The notion 'frame' refers to the way an activity is intended by the participants and the way their roles are understood within it (Tannen and Wallat 1987; quoted from De Fina 1997: 347). For example, if *well* occurs in the context of a narrative we can assume that it marks different stages of the narrative (cf. Norrick 2001). *Well* in this case functions as an instruction or cue to the hearer to interpret what follows in relation to common or shared knowledge about how a narrative is built up. Compare Gumperz: 'Co-participants who perceive and respond to the shift are then led to resort to their background knowledge and by an inferential process akin to Gricean implicature, to derive contextual presuppositions in terms of which the signs can be understood' (1996: 379–80).

Thus the description of *well* as a contextualisation cue explains why a conversational move introduced by *well* can be interpreted differently depending on the expectations associated with the particular speech activity where it is used. For example, in classroom lessons *well* is used to facilitate tasks such as indicating the opening of a lesson or showing whether the conversational turn is associated with the teacher or the student (cf. Chapter 2). In doctor-patient interviews the use in questions and answers is related to the interview format where the doctor asks questions and the patient provides information.

In the following example from a broadcast discussion, *well* has the function of signalling the introduction of a new speaker in the debate:

(1)   A: Melvyn Bragg you're President of the National Campaign for the Arts the lead
        signatory in the letter part of which I quoted a few moments ago
        What do you think's gone wrong <,>
        B: <u>Well</u> before we start to talk about finances which'll occupy a lot of this pro-
        gramme and blame which'll occupy a lot of this programme the reason why I'm
        we're here and people are watching is because most people think that the arts add
        something to their lives that nothing else will give them
        (S1B-022 0012–0014 BROADCAST DISCUSSION)

Pragmatic markers typically occur at transitions in the discourse where the hearer needs to be made aware that a new activity starts or that the speaker takes on a new role. On the metapragmatic level the hearer switches to making inferences on the basis of the interpretative 'debate frame' specifying that new speakers should be introduced by a moderator in the discussion.

However, many social events contain both 'fixed parts' which need to be interpreted according to a frame (such as the classroom frame or the telephone frame) and parts where speakers step out of their roles as 'teacher' or 'student' or 'caller' or 'answerer' in the telephone conversation. It follows that the hearer has to shift back and forth from interpreting what is said according to shared stereotypic knowledge to interpret what is said on the basis of general pragmatic rules drawing upon what is said to initiate a new utterance. Using a formulation from Silverstein we could say that 'there is no language use without a constant calibration between pragmatic and metapragmatic functioning' (Verschueren 2000: 445).

The use of contextualisation cues and interpretative frames to describe background knowledge needed for interpretation is not a new idea. According to Levinson (1979: 371), we need to consider 'inferential schemata tied to (derived from, if one likes) the structured properties of the activity in question'. In the following chapters we will use the term frame to refer to such 'inferential schemata'. These are needed to explain what pragmatic markers contribute to the interpretation of the discourse.

1.3 Methodology

Corpus studies of pragmatic markers in different varieties of English are still fairly new. Studies of pragmatic markers in different types of activity such as courtroom examinations, the classroom, and other task-oriented dialogues have mostly been based on data collected by the researcher him- or herself. In such an approach, the use of observation and ethnographic fieldwork data goes hand in hand with control of the data which is difficult to achieve by other means. Corpora, on the other hand, provide many advantages if we want to compare pragmatic markers in different text types (activities and regional varieties).

Luckily there now exist many new corpora and these make it possible to compare pragmatic markers both across text types and across regional and social varieties. As Mair (2009: 8) has pointed out, 'the rapidly growing number of publicly available corpora of English combine an increasing amount of material which sociolinguists would disregard at their peril.' Below I will discuss the possibilities of using many different corpora to study how pragmatic markers depend on factors such as such as text type, regional variety, and changes over time.

My main resource has been the ICE-GB Corpus (the British Component of the International Corpus of English).[1] The ICE-GB Corpus was collected within a project aiming at documenting varieties of English on a regional basis and is therefore also suitable for making comparisons with other regional varieties (see also Chapter 4).

Corpora make it possible to make quantitative and qualitative observations about the function of pragmatic markers, their position in the utterance and the discourse, as well as their collocations and prosody. A special advantage with the ICE-GB corpus is that it can be used as a 'sociolinguistic corpus'. It represents a wide range of spoken and written text types and makes it possible to study pragmatic markers in many situations and with a variety of speakers in different social roles. The corpus is small (one million words) in comparison with other existing corpora but has a fairly large spoken component (600,000 words) collected between 1990 and 1993. Since pragmatic markers occur mainly in speech, I have concentrated on the spoken data from the ICE-GB Corpus. However, in analysing *actually* and *in fact* I will also refer to the frequencies in the written part of the corpus. The wide coverage of text types makes it possible to show both where a particular marker occurs and where it does not occur. The largest material in the spoken corpus represents informal conversation ('private dialogue') which may be explained by the fact that this is the most interesting text type for studying spoken phenomena. However pragmatic markers need to be studied in many more text types. As Lam points out, there are few studies of pragmatic markers across social situations or text types although we can expect pragmatic markers to do quite different things depending on who uses them and for what purposes (Lam 2009).

In the ICE-GB the general categories are, for instance, private dialogue and public dialogue. Public dialogue consists of classroom lessons, broadcast discussions, broadcast interviews, parliamentary debates, legal cross-examinations and business transactions. Not all categories are self-explanatory. Legal presentation refers for example to the presentation of a legal case by an attorney in court. Spontaneous commentaries consist both of sports commentaries and commentaries on public events.

Categories such as broadcast discussion or classroom lesson may be considered 'speech events' (Hymes 1972), 'social situations' (Ochs 1996) or activity types (Levinson 1979). Activity types can differ with regard to topic, speakers, the relationship between speakers, purpose, etc. The present study will focus on some activities represented by the texts in the ICE-GB.

An advantage of the ICE-GB corpus is that it is possible to listen to the spoken recordings accompanying the texts. The prosodic contextualisation features which are of interest to the study of pragmatic markers include prosody, accent and intonation but also rhythm, pace of delivery, loudness and related phenomena such as pausing, overlaps and repetition. Both prosody and pronunciation can be assumed to be a part of the patterns associated with the speakers' shared knowledge about the use of the markers. *Well,* for example, is pronounced both with and without a full vowel. However, the examples have not been transcribed and I have had to rely on my own prosodic analysis of the data.

In order to study pragmatic markers such as *and that sort of thing* and *or something* and their formal and functional varieties in different regional varieties I have used some of the ICE Corpora which are available (see Chapter 4). Recent changes in the use of pragmatic markers can be studied in the Diachronic Corpus of Present-Day Spoken English (DCPSE). The DCPSE Corpus compares data from the London-Lund Corpus (LLC) of Spoken English (mainly from the 1960s and 1970s) with similar texts from the ICE-GB Corpus. Ongoing changes and new uses of the pragmatic markers can also be studied in the conversations among London adolescents in the COLT Corpus (the Bergen Corpus of London Teenagers) (cf. Chapter 2, footnotes 4 and 5).

1.4 Linguistic theories accounting for the relationship between pragmatic markers and context

All utterances are embedded in a social, cultural and linguistic context. What makes pragmatic markers unique is that they 'allow context into the linguistic analysis' (Verschueren 1999: 111). Not surprisingly, pragmatic markers can therefore be regarded as a testing ground for contextual theories of meaning. '[I]n different varieties of pragmatic theory, from Relevance Theory to more conservative Gricean theories, current work is addressed to explaining how almost vacuous or semantically general expressions can have determinate interpretations in particular contexts' (Gumperz and Levinson 1996: 8). The situation is characterised by a tension between theories focusing on the use of pragmatic markers 'when people talk to each other' and theories focusing on their production and understanding as a cognitive ability. According to Blakemore (2002: 5), for instance, 'the object of study [in pragmatics] is not discourse, but the cognitive processes underlying successful linguistic communication, and the expressions which have been labelled as discourse markers must be analysed in terms of their output to those processes.' A theory of the latter kind is relevance theory.

In this section I will review several theories describing how meaning is created in or interacts with the context. Integrative theories (1.4.1) describe systematic relationships between language and context on many different levels. Relevance theory will be described in Section 1.4.2. and the theory of meaning potentials in Section 1.4.3. The theory of meaning potentials will be further developed in Chapter 2 where I argue that the meaning of *well* is not fixed but *well* can best be described as having a maximally rich meaning or meaning potential, part of which is activated in the situation.

1.4.1 Integrative theories

'Integrative' theories provide a rich description of what pragmatic markers are doing in the discourse. Starting with Schiffrin's pioneering study of 'discourse markers' (1987), the functions of pragmatic markers were analysed with regard to the structure of the discourse and more recent studies have all acknowledged the close relationship between discourse structure and pragmatic markers. Schiffrin starts out with the assumption that:

> Not only does language always occur in a context but its patterns – of form and function, and at surface and underlying levels – are sensitive to features of that context . . . In sum I assume that language is potentially sensitive to all of the contexts in which it occurs, and even more strongly, that language **reflects** those contexts because it helps to constitute them. (Schiffrin 1987: 4)

Schiffrin defined discourse markers operationally as 'sequentially dependent elements which bracket units of talk' (1987: 31) and attempted to 'describe in a systematic way the discourse in which markers occurred' (ibid. 312). A number of different dimensions are distinguished making it possible to describe the multifunctionality of the markers (ibid. 24f.). Discourse is viewed as 'action' constrained by linear sequence (e.g. what precedes and what follows), the participation framework (the relationship between speaker/hearer and between speaker/utterance). Turns are constituted through the exchange structure (the sequentially defined structure also known as adjacency pair). Other 'structures' in Schiffrin's model have to do with information state (who has access to knowledge and what is shared knowledge) and the ideational structure (e.g. topic relations or cohesive relations). All markers have indexical functions. *Well,* for instance, indexes the utterance to the speaker (and to the hearer) and to the prior or upcoming text.

Schiffrin's model has been important for the present work; for example, in the attention to many different aspects of the communication situation and the importance of indexicality and deixis to explain the role of pragmatic markers in the context. Schiffrin describes her model as 'integrative' since it involves multiple contextual components which contribute to the overall sense of 'the coherence' of discourse.

Östman does not describe his model as 'integrated' or 'integrative'. However, it is also an attempt to view pragmatic markers from more than one perspective (Östman 1995). According to Östman, communication does not operate according to Rationality principles (such as the relevance principle) but according to 'Common Sense' principles, which need their own analytical tool box (ibid. 106). Pragmatics (in a broad sense) provides us with the 'parameters and potential values' that linguistic elements have when they are looked at from a pragmatic perspective, for example, with regard to society, discourse, culture, human relationships (ibid. 107). This model is also compatible with the pragmatic markers being ambivalent or variable in meaning – 'a both-and manifestation'. They have values with regard to all the parameters. However, a certain 'value' can be highlighted (foregrounded) or backgrounded in the communication situation. Östman's model will be further discussed in Section 1.7 and in more detail in Chapter 2 since it provides the functional typology I have used to analyse *well*.

1.4.2 Relevance theory

Blakemore regards relevance theoretic pragmatics as having the 'potential to provide a theory of utterance interpretation which is consistent with generative grammar' (Blakemore 2002: 7). The contribution of relevance theory would be to explain the role of inference for utterance interpretation while generative grammar provides an account of the coding-decoding mechanism in communication. Let us consider how relevance theory can be applied to the multifunctionality of *well* (cf. Chapter 2, Section 2.2).

Relevance theory accounts for the 'frustrating elusiveness' of *well* associated with its changing purposes by referring to a communicative principle of relevance which allows the hearer to infer the intended interpretation. A pragmatic marker such as *well* can be viewed as a signal from the speaker allowing the hearer to make the assumptions required to recover an interpretation consistent with the guarantee of optimal relevance (every act of ostensive communication communicates a presumption of relevance). Relevance theory takes a hearer perspective and regards pragmatic markers as a signal to the hearer to take an inferential route. According to Blakemore (2002: 47)[2], *well* could be regarded as a signal simply in the sense that 'it provides a green light for the hearer, a sign to go ahead with the inferential process involved in the derivation of cognitive effects'. Thus Innes (2010), for example, refers to four different functions of *well* ('perceived needs') and suggests that the choice between them is made by the hearer on the basis of optimal relevance:

> Relevance theory may be a useful framework in that it can account for *well*'s different functions within the same account; that is, the structural (cohesion and delay) and attitudinal (including face and politeness) can be gathered under the umbrella of procedural encoding and optimal relevance. (Innes 2010: 115)

However, theories focusing only or mainly on finding a common principle explaining how the different functions of *well* can be inferred on the basis of contextual assumptions may not be sufficient to explain how *well* is interpreted in relation to the text type or the role of the speaker in the actual speech situation.

> [T]he possible effects arising from a number of linguistic and contextual factors on the use of discourse particles might be understated in such an approach [as relevance theory], and one of the crucial missing elements is the influence of text type in the interpretation of the pragmatic meanings of discourse particles. (Lam 2009: 354)

Relevance theory does not take 'an integrated view' on how utterance meaning is achieved and is therefore less adequate to describe what is going on in talk-in-interaction. In particular, it does not explain how pragmatic markers can change over time or in different text types. We need also to consider politeness principles and appropriateness conditions which are less general than the relevance principle but specific to a particular culture or society, region, social situation, historical period, etc.

1.4.3 Pragmatic markers and meaning potentials

It can be claimed that pragmatic markers do not have a fixed meaning but a meaning potential. The theory of meaning potential can cope with the meaning representation of lexical items which have no strictly delimited meanings but develop meanings in situated use (Norén and Linell 2007). According to Norén and Linell (2007: 387), the basic assumptions of a theory of meaning potentials are 'that the linguistic resources provide language users with semantic resources to understand, say and mean specific things in particular usage events, and that this always involves an interplay with contextual factors'.

The theory of meaning potentials provides a rich meaning description of pragmatic markers where the interaction with the context is important. According to Norén and Linell (2007: 390), '(a) theory of meaning potentials assumes that parts of a word's meaning are evoked, activated or materialised, foregrounded or backgrounded, *in different ways in the different contexts,* in which it is exploited.' Fischer, for example, found that different meanings of (the meaning potential of) *okay* were activated depending on whether the situation was human-to-computer communication or communication between humans. She found that speakers did not use *okay* to take their turn or play for time although these functions were frequent in communication with another human being (Fischer 2006: 441).

The theory of meaning potentials describes the relationship between meaning and context in a different way from relevance theory: 'the context selects the meaning of a pragmatic marker' whereas in relevance theory a pragmatic marker looks for a context which is compatible with communicative principles. If meaning is selected in the communication situation we need a description of the contextual factors which interact with the meaning potential of the lexical item. As will be shown in Section 1.5, the 'relevant' or selected context can include text type and speakers and related features such as speaker identities, professions, etc. which are indexed in the communicative situation along with discourse and pragmatic functions. In addition, formal features (the linguistic co-text) can be regarded as being part of the context (or usage domain).

The 'meaning potential' approach can also be compared with the rich description of the formal, functional and contextual aspects of pragmatic markers in a construction grammatical framework (Fried and Östman 2005; Östman 2006). Like constructions, meaning potentials represent part of the language user's knowledge of language. 'It seems rather that meaning potentials are part of the actors' knowledge of language, and they are used in the negotiation of situated interpretations' (Linell 1998: 82 quoted from Keevallik 2003: 32).[3] In particular, we can look upon meaning potentials as an economical way of storing the speaker's knowledge about language. We also need to consider how the information is stored. The meaning potential of pragmatic markers is not an unordered set of meanings but the 'potential' must have some internal structure. The theory is compatible with the polysemy of pragmatic markers, that is, the idea that pragmatic markers have one or several core meanings from which new functions can be created in the interaction. It has for instance been suggested that the meanings of *well* can be organised into '"two broad spaces": that of modal functions and that of structural functions' (Cuenca 2008: 1388). In

Cuenca's analysis *well* has a radial structure or semantic networks with more peripheral meanings organised around one of the core aspects. Meaning potentials organise (only) the conventionalised meanings of pragmatic markers. The conventionalised meanings are important because they can be the basis for classifying the pragmatic markers. They are distinguished from less conventionalised (or ad hoc) meanings created in the communication situation.

The theory of meaning potentials is compatible with what we know about how meanings can be negotiated, modified or changed diachronically (both in a short and a long time perspective). It can also explain what we know about how pragmatic markers are acquired. Children and language-learning novices first acquire pragmatic markers in prototypical face-to-face situations and then start using them in more situations and new contexts when they are socialised into new ways of life. It has, for instance, been shown that English-speaking children acquire the potential for systematic sociolinguistic variation together with pragmatic markers from an early age (Andersen et al. 1999: 1349).

Meaning potentials are potentially creative and 'make possible all the usages and interpretations of the word or construction that language users find reasonably correct, or plainly reasonable in the actual situations of use' (Norén and Linell 2007: 389). They can therefore explain how markers can be used in text-type specific or innovative ways in the communication situation. Greasley (1994), for example, investigated the use of *well* in television commentaries on the game of snooker and found that *well* was produced under certain contextual conditions such as 'a surprisingly good shot'. Since *well* is used we can assume that speakers experienced the situation as similar in some ways to prototypical situations where *well* is needed and therefore extended it to new situations.

To sum up, pragmatic markers have a variable and context-bound character. Their meaning therefore cannot be described in the same way as lexical elements which have a more stable lexical meaning. The theory of meaning potentials accounts for the fact that pragmatic markers get their meaning through 'dynamic sense-making' in local, situated contexts (Norén and Linell 2007). Finally, we should note that the theory of meaning potentials is appropriate to describe the different uses of pragmatic markers in new text types in the corpora. We can use it to explain both established or conventionalised meanings and innovative or ad hoc meanings characteristic of special activities.

1.5 Pragmatic markers and the context

Pragmatic markers get their meaning in interaction with the context. It is therefore important to define what is meant by context. Context needs to be taken in a broad sense. In the anthropological literature we find a rich description of the social situation (social event, activity type) which is relevant for the analysis of pragmatic markers. The description of the social dimensions below is based on Ochs (1996). Ochs suggests that linguistic elements can reach beyond the utterance and index elements such as the speaker, speaker identities and activity and especially the speaker's (epistemic and affective) stance.

The notion explaining the association between pragmatic markers and the context is assumed here to be indexicality. Indexicality has an entrenched position in the deictic systems associated with time, space and person in different languages. However, studies of deixis in different languages generally focus on structures or elements indexing a single situational dimension only. As a result, we know a great deal about adverbs and pronominal forms indexing dimensions such as the time and place of the activity or the speaker/hearer framework. In the sentence 'The book is here', *here* indexically shifts its interpretation depending on the place where the communication takes place.

In comparison with other deictic elements, the pragmatic markers have a rich social meaning since they are used to indexically refer to a number of 'speech act' features such as the speaker and the hearer, social identities and the speech event (social activity) itself.

> While a number of studies of language use dwell on the relation of linguistic forms to only one situational dimension and ignore social dimensions socio-culturally linked to that dimension, other studies . . . consider a range of situational dimensions socio-culturally entailed by a set of linguistic forms. (Ochs 1996: 418)

Ochs identifies the following socio-cultural dimensions of the communicative situation (other than time or place):

> *Social identity* encompasses all dimensions of social personae, including roles (e.g. speaker, overhearer, doctor, teacher), relationships (e.g. kinship, friendship), group identity (gender, generation, class, ethnic membership) and rank (employer and employee).
> *Social act* refers to a socially recognised goal-directed behavior (e.g. a request, an offer)
> *Activity* refers to a sequence of at least two social acts, e.g. disputing, interviewing[4]
> *Affective stance* refers to a mood, attitude, feeling, and disposition, as well as degrees of emotional intensity
> *Epistemic stance* refers to knowledge or belief vis-à-vis some focus of concern, including degrees of certainty of knowledge
> (quoted from Ochs 1996: 410 with some abbreviations)

An important dimension of the communicative situation is stance. Fischer (2006: 445) observes for example: 'Thus discourse particles [pragmatic markers] make the human interlocutors (with their hopes, fears, desires, and imperfections) part of the situation.' However it is not immediately obvious that pragmatic markers can express epistemic and affective stance. 'Less recognized is the fact that, in many languages, affective and epistemic stance is encoded at many levels of linguistic structure' (Ochs 1996: 412). Ochs's examples are sentential adverbs (disjuncts) and constructions with epistemic verbs (*I think*) which are closely associated with speakers and their feelings. Ochs does not discuss pragmatic markers but it can be argued that many of them have an important stance-marking function and that they can express a large number of stances depending on the text type.

A speaker confronts 'numerous possibilities in framing and executing her speech' and take up a stance depending on the preceding context and how they want to appear (Mertz and Yovel 2003: 6). Epistemic stance can be associated with uncertainty and politeness. In other cases, an element of disagreement or 'fighting' is conveyed by the lexical element. The component of 'fighting' is illustrated by the following example from Ochs (1996: 423), borrowed from M. H. Goodwin (1990) in which Ruby uses *I know* not (only) to express certainty but to 'construct a challenge to' Stacey's assumption that 'it's a free world' is news to him:

> Stacey: Fight yourself.
> Ruby: Well you make me fight myself.
> Stacey: I can't make you. Cuz it's a free world.
> Ruby: I know it's a free world.

Even agreeing with the preceding speaker can carry with it an element of 'fighting' or divergent opinion as shown by this example.

Pragmatic markers are contextual resources enabling speakers to express a number of new stances in the interaction. In particular, they can have a rhetorical function allowing the speaker to take up a stance of alignment or disalignment to the hearer or to what is said. It is easy to overlook the fact that pragmatic markers can also be used to express authority and power (an authoritative or knowledgeable stance) associated with a particular social or professional identity. As shown by Ochs, there is link between stance and social identity conveyed by cultural expectations. For example the speaker may display an authoritative stance in order to build up an identity as a medical doctor. However pragmatic markers are flexible and can be used with different stances and exhibit different speaker statuses depending on the social activity and the speaker role. *Well* can, for instance, be used by a prosecutor in a court examination to display an authoritative stance. If *well* is used by the witness, on the other hand, it is associated with a deferential attitude. In such examples (which will be further illustrated in Chapter 2), *well* does not merely point to a social identity but helps to constitute or construct that identity (Ochs 1996: 424). Affective stance is also important with pragmatic markers. *Well* can, for instance, signal disappointment, resignation or reluctance.

As will be further illustrated in the empirical studies, pragmatic markers have a rich situational meaning which is exploited in the communication situation also for the speaker's manipulative purposes. If one does not understand what roles pragmatic markers have in communication and how they vary their functions situationally, this can have serious consequences for example in court proceedings (Hale 1999). As Hale points out (cf. Chapter 2: Section 2.2), the translators (interpreters) often mistranslated *well* (in the prosecutor's questions) or omitted it from their translation which resulted in misunderstandings.

Let us note finally that even though there are many cues to the intended interpretation of pragmatic markers in the context we should not underestimate the problems of conveying or interpreting the situational meaning. The flexible and fuzzy meaning of pragmatic markers places a burden on both the speaker and the hearer in the communication situation. The speaker must have access to a large number of linguistic and extra-linguistic conventions in order to use pragmatic markers. Hearers use a number of clues such as the lexical meaning, grammatical features (such as position or collocation), gestures and prosody to interpret the situation meaning of pragmatic markers.

Even so, misunderstandings are common. According to Ochs (1996: 413):

> [i]t is important to stress at this point that the assignment of situational meanings is a complex, interactionally accomplished process. Interlocutors have

available to them a reserve of linguistic structures – some grammatical, others discursive – that are conventionally associated with particular situational dimensions. Interlocutors may use these structures to index a particular identity, affect, or other situational meaning; however, others co-present may not necessarily assign the same meaning.

1.6 Formal features of pragmatic markers

As argued in Section 1.4.3, pragmatic markers can be regarded as lexical resources associated with 'a meaning potential'. They also have formal properties which are part of the description of their usage. These can be of different kinds: 'The more one studies discourse particles, the more conventions one discovers with regard to their use. The features are syntactic (e.g. position, prosodic, lexical (e.g. collocations) and stylistic (e.g. text type)' (Aijmer 2002: 28). However, few studies look at the formal features in detail, probably because it is difficult to establish a clear link between form and what pragmatic markers are doing in communication.

For example, pragmatic markers do not occur anywhere in the utterance or the turn but there are rules for their placement which also have to do with their function. In addition, sequential information is important. Pragmatic markers can point both backwards or forwards to project a new turn. They can also have a global textual function and point forwards to a narrative, argument or description. They occur in different linguistic contexts and can have different functions depending on whether they occur in questions or answers.

Prosodic (and other formal) features have been discussed as clues to the function of pragmatic markers and as criteria for their status as pragmatic markers. For example, in the area of speech recognition and understanding, pragmatic markers have been regarded as 'cue phrases' which together with prosodic and grammatical uses (such as position in the utterance) constitute important information for understanding how the utterance is segmented or to disambiguate its different meanings or functions (Hirschberg and Litman 1993; Horne et al. 2001).

The relationship between form, function and prosody is even more complicated if a pragmatic marker is multifunctional. At least in some cases we find interesting correlations between form and function. Ferrara's (1997) study of *anyway* is of particular interest in this respect. Ferrara established three different meanings or subtypes of *anyway* which could be distinguished on the basis of syntactic position and prosody.

Ferrara's analysis is compatible with the use of prosody as a 'cue' (along with other features) enabling the hearer to identify the function of a particular pragmatic marker in its context. However, not everything is conventionalised: '[. . .] prosodic choices [. . .] are motivated in part by convention, but largely by the often conflicting demands and constraints of the semantic, pragmatic and discoursal functions that discourse markers fulfil' (Wichmann et al. 2010: 150). It is obvious that formal features do not have a simple relationship to function. Thus, for example, a pragmatic marker in initial position (and a certain prosody) can be a cue to a discourse function (e.g. the use of a pragmatic marker to introduce a new topic). However, the same function may be fulfilled by other pragmatic markers which are placed initially and have a certain prosody (what Bazzanella 2006: 454 refers to as their (partial) interreplaceability). Fischer (2006: 443) gives examples of how *okay, hmm, oh* or *well* can all function to 'signal successful perception, understanding and topic continuity' although they do it in different ways. Both interreplaceability and the examples where it fails must be accounted for. The hypothesis here is that many different factors are involved in describing why a certain pragmatic marker is used. These factors include for example the speaker's knowledge that a pragmatic marker is associated with a certain text type, is used by a speaker in power, etc. In Chapter 3 on *actually* and *in fact*, it will be shown that even pragmatic markers which sometimes 'collide' in a particular function are associated with different usage conventions and can be experienced differently.

1.7 Functional features of pragmatic markers

The distinction between two or more basic functions of pragmatic markers is made in many functional models. A controversial issue is however how many parameters (domains, basic functions) we should distinguish. Fischer (2006: 430) considers a wide range of functions that pragmatic markers (Fischer's discourse particles) can have:

> Although scholars disagree much about the functions of discourse particles, there is a range of functions that is commonly, and often cumulatively, attributed to them. This spectrum includes functions with respect to the turn-taking system, the indication of discourse relations, discourse structuring, the regulation of interpersonal relationships, speech management, or politeness.

Schiffrin's 'integrative' proposal involving five different discourse planes was discussed in Section 1.4.1. However, many proposals distinguish fewer dimensions. Brinton (1996 and 2008) distinguishes two rather than three major functions. Pragmatic markers serve a textual function related to the structuring of discourse as a text and an interpersonal function 'which relates to the expression of speaker attitude and to the organization of the social exchange' (Brinton 2008).

Östman distinguishes three parameters 'in accordance with which communication takes place' (1995: 104) and 'with reference to which research into implicit pragmatics is doable': 'For me, then, discourse marking or discourse organizing is one major function that pragmatic particles have: a good candidate for another major function would be interaction-signalling; and yet another would be attitude/involvement signalling' (Östman 1995: 99).

We will return to Östman's functional typology in Chapter 2, where it is used to subclassify the functions of *well*.

1.8 Summary and conclusion

In this introductory chapter I have emphasised the need for a new study of pragmatic markers which focuses on their uses in different social and regional varieties. It will be shown that pragmatic markers function very differently depending on text type, activity, speaker roles, regional variety, etc. I have also discussed the type of theoretical framework we need to describe pragmatic markers and some basic assumptions underlying my approach.

Pragmatic markers have been characterised as metalinguistic indicators which attend closely to what is happening in the communication situation and remark explicitly on aspects of the ongoing speech event. They are used to manage the speaker's moment-to-moment progression from one turn to another. This analysis is not sufficient to describe how they are used in different situations. It has been argued that they can also be used as contextualisation cues indexing a frame for the interpretation of a pragmatic marker such as *well* when it has specialised uses (discourse tasks). Speakers also make use of 'stance' to take up different positions to the hearer or to the text in the interaction.

Traditionally it has been assumed that the context referred to is the linguistic environment in which the pragmatic markers are used. However, pragmatic markers also have a number of innovative or *ad hoc* meanings depending on the speaker or the social activity in which they occur. Pragmatic markers have 'indexically rich' sociolinguistic or situational meanings. To explain these we may have to go beyond the constraints imposed by the need to be coherent, polite or to express emotions and feelings. They can be indexed to elements 'in the air' such as the speaker, the hearer, (epistemic and affective) stance, social identities and a social activity. The social or situational meaning can be indirect, for example when a pragmatic marker is used by the speaker to 'construct' a certain social identity or professional identity (for example, as a teacher or a doctor). In such cases, the explanation of the meaning of a pragmatic marker involves cultural expectations, for example, about power status in society.

When we consider how pragmatic markers are used in different text types it becomes difficult to maintain that they have a fixed meaning. It has been argued that pragmatic markers 'construct' meaning potentials based on their uses in many different varieties. The meaning potential is in constant flux and is used creatively in new situations. In the actual communication situation the meaning potential is used selectively and perhaps with *ad hoc* or innovative functions.

Pragmatic markers can be looked upon as combinations of formal and functional features and descriptions of the contexts in which they are used. The formal features include, for example, pronunciation, pausing, positioning, linguistic context, collocation. However, there is not a simple relationship between form and function as will become apparent in the empirical case studies in the following chapters.

Notes

1. See the website http://www.ucl.ac.uk/english-usage/ice# (accessed 4 October 2012).
2. *Well* has also been described in a relevance-theoretical approach by Jucker (1993), de Klerk (2005), and Innes (2010).
3. Keevallik's orientation is, however, interactional linguistics and Conversation Analysis. Interactional linguistics combines a constructional approach and Conversation Analysis (see Keevallik 2003). It has in common with the meaning potential approach that it favours a rich representation of the meaning of lexical items. According to Deppermann (2006: 59), '[i]t is in fact one of the central tenets of interactional linguistics to reconstruct the holistic interplay of syntax, semantics, prosody, pragmatics, multimodality, and sequential aspects of grammatical structures in conversation and to

account for the contingencies of the empirically given token in all their informational richness' (quoted from Imo 2009: 4; Imo's translation).

4. Other terms which are used in similar ways are activity type (Levinson 1979) and communicative activity type (Linell 2009).

2

The Pragmatic Marker *Well*

Well, the little words are often the most interesting. (Innes 2010: 95)

2.1 Introduction

Well is interesting not least because of its frequency in conversation:

> A: Why don't you uhm replace one of the back doors here and use the pane from
> C: <u>Well</u> they're rotten now Dad so one day you'll have to
> A: <u>Well</u> I'm just putting that off for as long as possible
> C: <u>Well</u> if I ever have to replace a <,> back door I shall do so
> (ICE-GB)

The speakers in this little dialogue preface their contributions to the conversation with *well*. *Well* is not a part of the propositional content but its function is to enable the hearer to interpret how what is said should be understood. *Well* as a turn-initiator is used with several different functions. In the example above, *well* is, for example, used by C (the son) to signal that he is unwilling to replace one of the back doors because it is rotten. The father (A) uses *well* in a defensive way (I'm putting it off for as long as I can). In the next turn the son uses *well* to indicate reluctant agreement (If I replace a back door I will use a pane to do so). The examples of *well* have in common that they make the speaker come alive by expressing his emotions and attitudes. Without *well* the interaction would sound abrupt or impoverished because of the absence of the speaker attitude.

Not surprisingly, *well* has received more attention than any other English pragmatic marker (Schourup 2001: 1026). It has functioned as the testing ground for different theoretical approaches to the study of pragmatic markers and it has been investigated by means of several methods. However, existing studies on *well* show little agreement on controversial questions such as whether *well* has meaning, the number of functions it has and what these functions are. There are also neglected topics, for example how the function of *well* is allied to speaker roles and identities or to activities and text types.

Well has the potential to mean different things depending on the context. Does *well* add anything to the interpretation of the context? If this is the case what meaning or meanings does it have? In the past *well* has mostly been studied in conversation. Another aim of this chapter is to extend the study of *well* to different text types and situations to get a better picture of its formal and functional properties. The following research questions will be asked: In what text types is *well* frequent and why? What formal properties does *well* have? Where is it infrequent? What functions does it have in different text types? Who uses *well*? How is it used to establish a social identity and role?

The analysis of the functions of *well* in different text types can also contribute to the analysis of pragmatic markers generally by drawing attention to the situational or contextual variables motivating the choice and function of *well*. Such variables may depend on the medium (the difference between face-to-face and telephone conversation), the difference between monologue and dialogue, the presence of a person in control of turn-taking and the topic-management, etc.

Well has earlier been investigated on the basis of the London-Lund Corpus by Svartvik (1980). However, Svartvik analysed *well* only in a small sample of conversational texts and it is now possible to use more recent corpora than the London-Lund Corpus. The more recent ICE-GB Corpus (the British Component of the International Corpus of English) has therefore been chosen for the study of *well* here (see Chapter 1).

The outline of this chapter is as follows. Section 2.2 reviews previous analyses of *well* focusing on studies of the marker in different text types. The distribution of *well* over different text types in the ICE-GB is presented in Section 2.3. The formal properties of *well* are discussed in Sections 2.4 and 2.5 (collocation). In Section 2.6 it is argued that *well* has a meaning potential rather than a fixed meaning. Section 2.7 introduces the functional typology and the parameters used for the classification. The functions are discussed under the headings coherence (Section 2.8), involvement (Section 2.9) and politeness (2.10). In Sections 2.11–2.13 *well* is discussed in some selected text types and situations. Section 2.14 contains the conclusion.

2.2 Previous studies of *well*

It is hardly possible to give an overview of the vast literature on *well*, particularly as research is now extending into new areas (cross-linguistic studies, *well* in learner language).[1] *Well* has been the subject of many theoretical approaches, for example, the coherence-based theory of Schiffrin (1987), relevance theory (Jucker 1993; Blakemore 2002; de Klerk 2005), dialogue game theory (Carlson 1984) and politeness theory (Watts 1989). These theories explain the uses of *well* with regard to a single principle (such as relevance, or politeness) or postulate a core meaning and formulate a 'rule' from which other functions can be derived. Carlson, for instance, attempts to 'make a simple rule for *well* work in a wide variety of cases' (Carlson 1984: 2) in a theory of dialogue games.

In one of the most influential studies of *well* Schourup argues for instance that *well* (in present-day English) can be regarded as a 'gestural' interjection indicating a relationship between a mental state or attitude and 'a vocal 'portrayal' of that state' (2001: 1050). Because it is also a lexical item (as in *he speaks well*) it differs from interjections such as *oh* or *ah* which have no 'lexical' correspondence[2]. A similar 'interjectional' analysis is represented in other work and is compatible with the analysis of pragmatic markers as metalinguistic indicators tracing the speaker's progression through the discourse (cf. Chapter 1, Section 1.2.1). According to Biber et al., the speaker is neither certain nor uncertain but is thinking about things, collecting his or her thoughts when using *well* (1999: 1086). Compare also Carter and McCarthy (2006: 152) who, however, regard *well* as a discourse marker: 'A main function of *well* as a discourse marker is to indicate that the speaker is thinking about things'. This understanding of *well* is also close to Carlson's definition of *well* as deliberative, which he defines as 'weighing alternatives in terms of acceptability in order to arrive at a decision' (1984: 86). In other words, *well* signals an ongoing mental process in which the speaker deduces or infers something on the basis of considering the alternatives in a particular situation.[3] However the analyses proposed by Schourup or Carlson are characterised by meaning minimalism: *well* has a single core meaning from which new meanings can be derived. This analysis will be contrasted below (Section 2.6) with a 'richer' meaning theory making it possible to distinguish between core aspects (sub-senses, inferences, connotations, indexical meanings).

Another problem is that multifunctionality may be understood too narrowly because only conversational data is considered. For example, neither Schourup nor Carlson discuss *well* in different social contexts where we can assume that *well* can signal many different things. *Well* has a large number of functions depending on the social situation (activity type), text type and speaker role in addition to the linguistic context or general features in the communication situation.

A preferable starting-point is therefore to study formal and functional properties in different text types without considering how the functions fit in with a description of 'what *well* means'. *Well* has a number of specialised functions derived from its association with a particular text type and situation (the type of activity, who the speaker is, etc). Taking a hint from studies of *well* in other text types than conversation we can assume that many functions of *well* are not only dependent on the lexical meaning of *well* and the linguistic context but depend on cultural conventions or norms and social dimensions of the speech situation.

For natural reasons, past research has tended to focus on 'the give-and-take of everyday talk' (Norrick 2001: 851) and the functional categories proposed are those associated with conversation. However, we are now also beginning to see a number of analyses of *well* in very different types of text (Hale 1999; Fuller 2003; Greasley 1994; Norrick 2001; Innes 2010). They raise questions about the adequacy of earlier studies of the functions of *well* based on conversational data only. Below I will review some works which are of interest for the present study of *well* because they give evidence for the rich meaning potential of *well*, and in particular because they show that we need to go beyond its discourse-structuring functions.

Green (2006) studied the importance of *well* (and other pragmatic markers) for the creation of a question-answer system which could be used for natural language processing. She was interested in *well* because it is typically attitudinal unlike markers such as *now, okay, and* and *but:*

> Functionally, two basic kinds of discourse particles can be distinguished; both are conversational. Attitudinal discourse markers, such as *well, uh, like, gosh, oh, OK, I mean* and *y'know* indicate something about how the speaker feels about what is being said [. . .] (Green 2006: 118)

On the other hand, there are structural discourse markers like sentence-initial uses of *now, OK, and, but* which speakers use to indicate a structural boundary in the discourse. (Ibid. 119)

Green's analysis is interesting both because of the experimental approach and because she pointed to the association between *well* and the attitude of the speaker which she explained with reference to face-to-face contact with another speaker. Initial experimental work had shown that although the interface to the program was given a human voice it still did not sound sufficiently natural and friendly. Green's research team therefore chose to work with discourse particles (pragmatic markers) 'because they interact minimally with the syntax of the sentence they are attached to, while conveying a lot of information about the state of mind of the speaker' (Green 2006: 121). The intended result was said to be 'the illusion of a mind behind the monitor screen that thinks and cares about the user whom it addresses' (Green, ibid.). The reasons for using *well* also include the linguistic context according to Green. *Well* was therefore studied in different contexts to find out how *well* adjusts to different conversational demands (e.g. whether the sentence is a question or a declarative sentence, the effect of position, etc.).

The experimental design of Green's study pinpointed the important link between the speaker's emotions and attitudes and the use of *well* in conversation. However, the distinction between attitudinal and structural is not so clear-cut as suggested by Green. *Well* can, for instance, be both attitudinal and structural with functions such as topic shift or indicating a boundary in the discourse. In some text types, as we shall see below, the structural function of *well* is even predominant. A further point is that *well* is not only 'friendly' but it also conveys attitudes such as authority and power as well as rudeness in contexts characterised by unequal speaker-hearer relationships.

Green's study is interesting also for the present analysis of *well*. Green only studied spontaneous conversation where *well* was typically associated with friendliness. However, depending on the situation and text type *well* can convey many different attitudes including hesitation or uncertainty but also feelings such as disappointment or reluctance. Indirectly *well* can be used to construct a certain identity, personality or social persona. The association with attitudes is an important feature of many analyses of *well* foreshadowed in the discussion of pragmatic markers and indexicality in Chapter 1.

Of particular interest for this study is that we are now beginning to see a number of sociopragmatic studies of pragmatic markers, that is, studies paying attention to their functions and variability in different social contexts. These studies suggest that *well* can express different attitudes and functions in different text types or activities. These studies also point to the importance of *well* to express status or stance relating to personality and professional identity.

Hale investigated interpreters' treatment of *well* (and other markers) in the courtroom. According to Hale (1999: 1350), pragmatic markers such as *well* add 'tone and force' to the utterance. *Well* (and *see*) was for instance shown to be frequent in lawyers' questions in cross-examinations 'as an assertive device, indicative of superior authority' (ibid. 59). The importance of *well* appeared when *well* was not rendered by the interpreter in the court examinations or when it was mistranslated. Omitting *well* is always at a cost since the marker adds information about the speaker's attitudes, which is important in order to understand the speaker's intentions and to avoid misunderstanding. When *well* was not translated in the court proceedings the style and manner of the lawyer and defendant were not expressed. Moreover, interpreters frequently chose a translation that altered the illocutionary force of the utterance and therefore affected the witnesses' experiences of what went on during the proceedings. Hale's study suggests that *well* has a meaning which goes beyond the discourse context. However, the function has to do with emotion and stance rather than with the discourse structure.

Another courtroom study is Innes (2010). Innes discussed the use of *well* in jury trials in New Zealand courtrooms. The study showed that the use of *well* depends on the user's roles and the social goals of the activity. *Well* was for instance used in challenging questions in the cross-examination by the lawyer and with a hedging function in the defendant's answer.

Norrick's study of oral narratives is of particular interest when we study pragmatic markers in different text types since it shows that the functions of *well* cannot be distinguished from aspects of the on-going activity where it is used. According to Norrick (2001: 849), the functions of *well* in oral narrative can be related to the conventions for story-telling and its highly coded sequentiality. In Norrick's words, *well* acts as 'a specifically narrative DM [discourse marker] keyed on expectations about the organization of stories' (ibid. 857). *Well* can for instance lead into beginnings and endings of oral narratives and mark a return to the main theme of the story ('the stage-marker or staging function'). Müller (2004) who analysed oral narratives based on a silent Chaplin movie came up with related categories such as 'move to story' and 'introducing the next scene'.[4]

Besides narratives and courtroom proceedings, classroom discourse has attracted considerable attention because of its clear structure. Sinclair and Coulthard (1975), in their pioneering research, have shown how classroom interaction is regulated by the activities in the classroom and the specific roles of teachers and students. *Well* has an important function to signal different stages of the interaction. *Well* could, for example, occur as a framing move in a conversational exchange in the opening of the classroom lesson or to mark the transition from one stage of the discourse to another. Sinclair and Coulthard's work has also been an inspiration for a study of (Spanish) pragmatic markers in the classroom by De Fina (1997).

De Fina (1997) was concerned with describing the functions of Spanish *bien* (a pragmatic marker with functions overlapping with *well*) in classroom discourse. In her study *bien* was seen to have two classroom specific functions (both of which were associated with the teacher and not with the students). 'Transitional' *bien* was for instance used by teachers to signal changes in classroom activities, while evaluative *bien* functioned as a feedback move. Both functions could be associated with the degree of control of the teacher in the interaction. The transitional use of *bien* occurred at transitions and boundaries in the discourse, for example, to indicate that one phase of the classroom activity is finished and there is a change to a new situation with a different alignment of speakers. De Fina (1997) also suggested that Gumperz's term 'contextualization cue' could be used to mark the role of the transitional *bien* to change or redefine the context (cf. Chapter 1, Section 1.2.1).

Fuller (2003) discussed pragmatic markers in interviews and showed that *well* was used more frequently (but not exclusively) by the interviewer than by the interviewee and that it was found in different patterns:

> The DMs [discourse markers] *oh* and *well* are used relatively infrequently in the interviews by the interviewees, but at high rates in these same interactions by the interviewers. Because the interviewees are playing the role of the speaker more than of the listener, they are not expected to offer as many responses to the contributions of the interviewer as they would in a symmetrical conversation. The interviewer, however, is primarily a listener and thus uses these response signals more frequently. (Fuller 2003: 43)

Greasley's study (1994) is unusual in that he studied *well* in television commentaries on snooker games. Greasley found previous conversation-based analyses of *well* incomplete or insufficient to account for *well* in his data and suggested that contextual conditions prompting the commentator to use *well* involved the players' deliberations and actions in problematic situations in the game. In order to explain how the specialised functions of *well* in the television commentary are interpreted Greasley suggested that there may be a similarity between apparently different functions of *well*. For example, there is a similarity between problematic situations displayed in the snooker game which require the commentator to modify what has been said and situations requiring the speaker's modification of his or her own speech (1994: 492). Greasley concludes from his study that we need to go beyond looking for the core (or the etymological) meaning of *well* to consider more peripheral aspects (1994: 493):

> In the final analysis, however, since our use of the particle *well* is learnt through observing its use by others in situations such as those documented throughout this article, any reference to its etymological origins becomes rather abstract with regard to informing its current, pragmatic usage.

These studies show that a large number of contextual elements contribute to the frequency of *well* and its interpretation. These factors are, for instance, the speaker role (e.g. teacher–pupil, interviewer–interviewee) and indirectly who has authority or power in an asymmetric communication situation (interview, court proceedings), the formality of the speech situation (e.g. if the speakers are strangers or friends), conventions or rules for the activity (the rules for the snooker game, storytelling conventions) and its overall organisation.

2.3 Distribution of *well* in the corpus

Well is one of the most frequent pragmatic markers. It is less frequent than *oh* or *yeah* but more common than *you know* or *I mean* in British and American English according to Biber et al. (1999: 1096). Moreover, *well* is more frequent in American English than in British English (ibid. 1096). However, it is possible that it is losing its popularity. A comparison with the London-Lund Corpus (compiled in the 1960s and the 1970s) shows that it is less frequent in the more recent ICE-GB Corpus (3,143 examples in the LLC to be compared with 2,418 occurrences in the ICE-GB Corpus).[5] We can speculate that *well* sounds middle-aged and old-fashioned unlike for instance *like* or *okay*. This is also suggested by a comparison with the Bergen Corpus of London Teenage Language (the COLT-Corpus) (2,283 examples to be compared with 3,143 in the LLC).[6]

The frequencies for *well* include uses where *well* is not a pragmatic marker (*may/ might as well, he speaks well* and the unrelated noun). In the ICE-GB 173 out of 200 examples (conversation only) were used as pragmatic markers (86.5%).The results are similar to those of other studies. Romero-Trillo (2002: 777) found that 87.4% of the examples were pragmatic markers in a sample of 50,000 words from the LLC (439/502) and Stenström (1990a: 162) established a 'D-item ratio' of 86% for *well* when she looked at the whole LLC (2675/3103 examples). Lam (2006: 101) states that 'more than eighty per cent [of the uses of *well* in a corpus of talk shows] were used as a discourse particle'.[7]

Depending on the text type the pragmatic marker *well* is found with different frequencies (and functions). Table 2.1 shows how *well* is distributed over different text types.

Table 2.1 The distribution of the pragmatic marker *well*[8] in different text types in the spoken part of the ICE-GB Corpus. The frequencies have been normalised to 1,000,000 words. The text types where *well* is most frequent are in bold.

	Frequencies	Normalised frequencies	Number of words
Private (dialogue)			**205,608**
Direct conversation	1,290	**6,965**	185,193
Telephone calls	203	**9,943**	20,415
Public (dialogue)			**171,059**
Classroom lessons	149	3,530	42,208
Broadcast discussions	130	2,959	43,921
Broadcast interviews	82	3,702	22,147
Parliamentary debates	27	1,274	21,060
Legal cross-examinations	52	2,455	21,179
Business transactions	116	**5,646**	20,544
Unscripted monologues			**152,835**
Spontaneous commentaries	72	1,695	42,472
Unscripted speeches	32	4,843	66,065
Demonstrations	25	1,108	22,563
Legal presentations	9	414	21,735
Mixed			**42,962**
Broadcast news	45	1,047	42,962
Scripted monologues			**65,098**
Broadcast talks	32	735	43,506
Non-broadcast speeches	9	416	21,592

Well was mainly used in spoken language. In the ICE-GB corpus the only written text types where it occurred were fiction (10 examples) and social letters (42 examples). In social letters the function of *well* can be compared with conversation (the expression of friendliness) but there were also specific textual functions such as closing formulas (*well I had better sign off, oh well end of letter now, well that's all my news, oh well I suppose I ought to go to bed*).

Well is dialogic in nature as seen by its higher frequency in dialogue than in monologue. It was generally more frequent in unscripted than in scripted monologues. There may also be differences within a single category. In unscripted monologues there are quantitative differences between (spontaneous) commentaries and (unscripted) speeches which need to be explained. *Well* was infrequent in legal presentation (summaries by the judge before the jury convenes). This should be compared with scripted monologues where *well* was generally more infrequent than in unscripted ones.

Well was most frequent in conversation (face-to-face and especially telephone conversation), that is, in more informal types of situations characterised by intimacy and the close relationship between the participants. It was also frequent in business transactions, in classroom lessons and in interviews, that is, in public types of dialogue. However, the functions of *well* in these text types are only obvious from a closer analysis. The large number of examples in telephone conversations may be explained by the fact that speakers do not see each other and therefore use *well* as a signal that they are holding the line or taking their turn. *Well* can also compensate for the absence of body language and gestures (cf. Section 2.11.2). In spontaneous commentaries on different sports events, on the other hand, *well* was primarily used as an accompaniment to the moment-by-moment progression of the game (see Section 2.13).

Conversational data illustrate a wide variety of the uses of *well* and are a good starting-point for analysing its functions. When we look at other text types we need to consider 'specialised' or innovative uses of *well* which are motivated by features of the text type such as the social goal of an activity, who the speakers are, etc.

I have selected face-to-face conversation, telephone conversation, broadcast discussion, cross-examination and spontaneous commentary as typical representatives of different text types. A sample of 200 examples was used for face-to-face conversation (fewer examples are analysed in the other text types where *well* was less frequent). To begin with I will discuss the formal properties of *well*. As pointed out in Chapter 1, the formal features of pragmatic markers have generally been neglected perhaps because there has been a tendency to consider pragmatic markers to be 'a functional category' rather than combinations of functions and form. Another reason for this omission may be that there is not a simple relationship between form and function. Formal features may be associated with the functions of pragmatic markers in partly systematic, partly idiosyncratic ways. Although it has generally been admitted that there are relations between form and function, we know for example very little about how prosodic features are related to the functions of pragmatic markers. However, both formal and functional features are resources speakers rely on to convey their message.

2.4 Formal properties of *well*

Well has grammatical, semantic and prosodic properties in addition to its functional properties. The information could be integrated in constructions, that is, as combinations of form and (discourse) function incorporating the speakers' knowledge about the use of a particular marker (cf. Chapter 1, Section 1.4). According to Fried and Östman, 'different traditional "levels" of grammatical description (phonology, syntax, semantics, prosody, pragmatics, discourse, etc.) are integrated in a single complex sign – *a grammatical construction* – which represents a generalisation about speakers' grammatical knowledge' (2005: 1754).

However, *well* is flexible; it has the capacity to be used in new senses in new linguistic contexts and situations. This is not clear from Fried and Östman's definition. Secondly, the association between formal features and function is complex and involves frequencies. Thirdly, although the relationship between form and function is important we also need to consider the influence of the social situation in order to get a complete picture of the speakers' grammatical knowledge.

Below I will discuss the properties of *well* which we need to include in the description of its usage and if possible relate to function. Position plays an important role since initial position is closely linked to the definition of pragmatic marker (in its discourse-marking functions). De Klerk (2005: 1190), for example, regards initial position as the unmarked one for the discourse marker *well*: 'this tendency of *well* to precede utterances could generally be regarded as natural, since discourse markers typically act as a guide to addressees as to how to react to what is about to be said, rather than acting retrospectively on what has already been said.' The turn-initial position is not associated with a single function, however. Moreover, as will be shown below, *well* is also found within the turn with functions related to pausing or word-search.

Besides position prosodic factors play an important role. *Well* can for instance be pronounced in several ways. *Well* occurs in a 'full' version with the vowel pronounced as well as in the reduced form *w'l*. In addition, there is an 'extreme' reduced form which could be represented as 'W' (i.e. as schwa) where *well* may be difficult to distinguish from other pause markers (cf. Bolinger 1989: 333). The idea of focusing on the pronunciation of *well* rather than the intonation comes from Bolinger (1989). Bolinger (following Svartvik 1980) is pessimistic about starting the discussion of the prosody of *well* with intonation since we might be 'tempted to read in the intonational meaning as if it were the meaning of the interjection itself' (Bolinger 1989: 332). Bolinger suggests that 'a better place to start the discussion of the prosody of *well* is with accent rather than profile'. Svartvik, for instance, noted that 44% of the examples in his corpus were unaccented and 56% accented. However, as Bolinger suggested, 'but to test the possibility of a semantic contrast accompanying the process of reduction, it will be easier to compare full *well* and the fully reduced *w'l*' (1989: 333). In the study below I have distinguished between examples with a full vowel (sometimes without a following consonant) in the pronunciation and examples at the other end of the continuum where the vowel has disappeared.

It is important to study both prosody (including phenomena such as tempo and loudness) and accent (or whether the pronunciation of *well* is reduced) here because of their potential interest as cues to what happens in the communication situation as suggested by Gumperz:

> [. . .] prosody and 'accent' (in the sense of phonetically marked features of pronunciation) are among the principal means by means of which we identify where people are from and 'who' they are –that is assess their social identity. (1996: 366)

Tempo and loudness will be referred to in the individual examples since they contribute to the meaning of *well*, for example, its emotional connotations in different text types. A more ambitious project would be to study the prosodic features in more detail, for example, with regard to intonation.

Moreover, pausing plays an important role. *Well* was used with unfilled pauses both before (most frequent) and after the marker (with different frequencies depending on the text type). It also frequently co-occurred with pauses such as *uh(m)*, *I don't know*. Stenström notes that *well* has been 'found with long and complex pauses more often than other VF [verbal filler] categories', which points to its use as a 'staller' (with the function of expressing hesitation or consideration) rather than as a 'response initiator signalling "insufficiency"' (Stenström 1990b: 223). However, co-occurrence with pausing can be an unreliable cue to function. Moreover, when *well* was not accompanied by filled or unfilled pauses delay (stalling) is not the only possible function. 'We can justifiably attribute other functions to *well* in such examples' (Innes 2010: 106). The delay function may even be overridden by other functions. This is compatible with its being regarded as a core function from which other functions can be derived.

2.5 *Well* and collocation

Well has certain salient or prototypical meanings which are categorised according to certain parameters. However, for a more fine-grained analysis of the extended meanings of *well* the importance of collocations cannot be underestimated. As a result of co-selection two elements can become associated with each other and reciprocally constrain each other's interpretation. As Linell (2009: 322) points out, '[l]inguistic resources are often *co-selected* in discourse. Such resources will often mutually influence what aspects of their meaning potentials are reinforced in the situational utterance.' The corpus can help us to capture some of the collocations which are possible with *well*. For instance, *well* frequently collocated with elements such as o*kay*, *now*, *at least*, *anyway* where the collocate contributes to the interpretation of *well*. We can assume that collocations (the co-selection of *well* and another marker or construction) are documentations of past changes undergone by *well* which are more or less conventionalised. The collocations of *well* may also differ depending on the text type and situation and are an important cue to situational meanings. According to Fuller (2003: 25), speakers use 'stacking' (the combination of pragmatic markers such as *well, now*) 'to portray an authority figure such as a doctor.'

2.6 *Well* and meaning potentials

The starting-point for investigating the functions of *well* in the present study is corpus-driven and 'bottom-up'. The corpus-driven approach leads to the discovery of numerous more or less different functions of *well* depending on the linguistic and discourse context. Moreover, the number of new functions are multiplied if we go beyond conversation.

The project of accounting for the different uses of *well* can only be disappointing if the number of functions is not constrained in some way. Different theories have been proposed to account for the multifunctionality of *well* with this aim in focus (see Section 2.2). It has for instance been suggested that it has a core meaning which is underspecified (relevance theory) and becomes enriched in the context (e.g. Jucker, Blakemore) (see Chapter 1, Section 1.4.2). Other linguists have suggested that it has a core or a prototypical meaning from which other uses can be derived (e.g.Schourup, Carlson; Section 2.2). However there is very little agreement about issues such as *well*'s meaning and how we should account for its multifunctionality.

The theory of meaning potentials (Chapter 1, Section 1.4.3) implies 'a kind of compromise' or the description of an intermediate level between a more abstract meaning representation (a core meaning) and actual uses. In this theoretical approach *well* (and other pragmatic markers) does not have a fixed meaning but a meaning potential which is available as a communicative resource to language users. *Well* does not have a single core meaning (cf. Schourup and Carlson) but the theory provides a description allowing for several different core aspects (conventionalised meanings or 'sub-senses') from which new functions can be derived in the communication situation. Norén and Linell (2007) have discussed the meaning potential of words like *new* (Swedish 'ny') with a clear lexical meaning and how idiomatic uses (sub-senses) of the adjective are exploited in Swedish (*new and new*, Swedish 'ny och ny'). However, *well* seems to have little lexical meaning in comparison with 'ny' (new) or with other pragmatic markers such as *actually* or *in fact*.

In the next section I will suggest that *well* has distinct core aspects (sub-senses) corresponding to different perspectives 'in accordance with which communication takes place' (Östman 1995: 104). *Well* has core meanings (or sub-senses) associated with coherence, involvement and politeness.

In addition, *well* has functions which become visible only if we look at different social situations (activity types) where it occurs. When we describe how *well* is used, for example, for opening a discussion, challenging, hedging, or modification, the uses or functions are the result of the participants' negotiation and communicative work in concrete situations. We shall see, for example, that contextual factors associated with a particular text type can lead to the favouring of a specific use of *well*'s meaning potential.

2.7 Classification of *well* in this work

There are many possible ways of 'tackling the functions of pragmatic markers' (García Vizcaíno and Martínez-Cabeza 2005). The sociologically oriented Conversation Analysis (CA) has, for instance, been used to describe the contextual functions of *well* in terms of social action (e.g. whether the discourse is a broadcast discussion) and *well*'s sequential position in the discourse (Innes 2010). *Well* can, for instance, be described in terms of its position in the first or second part of an adjacency pair. The functions of *well* are established in the 'local talk-in-interaction'; for example the uses of *well* to signal feedback to a preceding utterance and to point forwards to the following turn. However, it is not possible to account for such functions of *well* as repair or hedging in terms of sequentiality. Moreover, it is difficult to make generalisations about what *well* is doing in different contexts (cf. Fischer 2000: 53). CA methods would for instance regard functions which could be related in other frameworks such as *well* in closings and *well* in openings as unrelated. The meaning potential approach, on the other hand, stresses the importance of conventionalised meanings which are part of the speaker's grammatical knowledge.

Conversational Analysis draws attention to dialogic aspects of pragmatic markers in the communication situation. In addition to functions which are derived from the sequential organisation involved in turn-taking we need to distinguish functions which are oriented to other and more general contextual parameters or domains. For the purposes of this work I have looked at models which postulate major functions 'from above'. I will choose Östman's (1995) classification to describe how the conventionalised uses of *well* are organised.

According to Östman, pragmatics (in a broad sense) provides us with the 'parameters and potential values' that linguistic elements have when they are looked at from a pragmatic perspective' (Östman 1995: 107), for example, with regard to society, discourse, culture and human relationships. This model provides a starting-point for generalising about *well*. It is also compatible with the pragmatic markers being ambivalent or variable – 'a both-and manifestation'. *Well* can have values with regard to all the parameters as we will see below. However, a certain 'value' can be highlighted (foregrounded) or back-grounded in the communication situation. This is compatible with the flexibility and variability of *well* which can be exploited in the communication situation: a certain function can be activated and others back-grounded depending on the social act, who the speaker is, position in the utterance, etc.

Östman (1995) defines the functions of pragmatic markers in general in terms of three very general meanings or parameters. His analysis therefore has certain advantages over Schiffrin's (1987) functional model where the planes are discussed 'only in terms of marker options' and not in terms of communication in general (see Redeker 1991: 1167). However, there are similarities both with Schiffrin's taxonomy discussed in Chapter 1, Section 1.4.1 and with Brinton's classification into textual and interpersonal functions (Chapter 1, Section 1.7). A difference is that the possible perspectives or parameters in Östman's model are few in comparison with those suggested by Schiffrin (1987) who distinguished five different 'discourse planes' to which pragmatic markers could be indexed.[9]

When choosing the relevant parameters (and the number of parameters) I was also influenced by Pichler (2010: 599) who suggests that, 'for quantitative purposes, models with fewer domains might be preferable, though'. Moreover even if the model is parsimonious it allows us to draw as many distinctions as are necessary for the description of their use (ibid. 599) and distinguishing more precise senses.[10]

According to Östman, pragmatic markers have functions with regard to social or discourse coherence (related to social conventions and norms, building the discourse by providing the 'grease' between parts of discourse), speaker's active involvement in the interaction (emotions and attitudes) and politeness (both with the establishment of interpersonal relations and breaking them, i.e. with impoliteness).[11]

However, the functions suggested are not watertight and *well* can be classified in different ways: 'It can be debated which constraints should be grouped under which domain, but that is only in the nature of things—that is how language works' (Fried and Östman 2005: 1760). Another problem is that *well* can have several functions simultaneously ('mixed' functions; Imo 2009, unpublished). In a theory of meaning potentials this can be expected. Depending on the topic, social situation and sequentiality several different functions of *well* can be activated.

The three parameters correspond to an abstract representation of the meaning of *well* in the sense that they constrain the uses of *well*. A few examples will be given of *well* in different core functions (sub-senses) oriented to these parameters in Sections 2.8–2.10. The examples are mainly from conversation. When we look at more text types other uses of *well* will be discussed.

2.8 *Well* and coherence

I regard coherence as a property which is achieved in the discourse by means of pragmatic markers (and in other ways). Coherence markers 'can well be regarded as the main organizers of discourse' (Östman 1995: 104). They are 'the grease' between the propositional parts of discourse making it work as discourse and they can create coherence 'locally' within the speaker's turn. The following 'micro-functions' (sub-senses) have been distinguished:

- word search and self-repair
- projecting a new turn
- transition according to an agenda
- transition to a quotation

2.8.1 Word-search and self-repair

Well in this function is closely associated with consideration, deliberation, hesitation and is used to gain time for cognitive processes 'connected with prompting of memory, search of memory, hesitation and planning' (Allwood et al. 1990: 11). This function has also been associated with 'stalling' and 'delay' (cf. Section 2.4). *Well* co-occurs with pauses or with phrases such as *I guess* or *I don't know*. However, *well* does more than simply fill a pause. In the following example from my corpus material *well* (*I guess*) is the outward manifestation of the speaker's 'weighing how much to say or deciding what propositions need to be articulated to convey an idea' Green (2006: 123). It reflects an ongoing cognitive process where the speaker is trying to think about examples of physical activities which are suitable for disabled persons:

(1)   A: What sort of activities physical activities were available
      B: Well I suppose uhm the <,> the standard kind of physiotherapy <,> when
      you asked for it <,> uhm <,> and well sports I guess <,>
      But <,> I mean I'm not necessarily interested in doing sports
      and just because I became disabled <,> it doesn't mean to say that I suddenly
      had a surge of interest in <,> going to play <,> uhm I don't know basketball or
      anything <,>
      (S1A-003 002–005 FACE)

(*And*) *well* co-occurs with (filled and unfilled) pauses and is pronounced with a falling tone.
   In (2) *well* signals that the speaker has found the right expression:

(2)   A: One's about the human brain and language And the other's about uh this guy
      called Chomsky who's uh <,,> well one of the world's most important human
      beings if you happen to be interested in linguistics
      (S1A-092 102–103 TELEPHONE)

Well here is lengthened and pronounced with a relatively high pitch and is accompanied by laughter.

Well can be used together with false starts or to revise an error in the preceding discourse. The speaker's problems are also evidenced by pausing and repetition. In the example below, the speaker stops midway and then starts again using *well*:[12]

(3) B: <u>Uhm Uhm Well I Well I</u> think it's
     Uhm <unclear-word> <,> in the early stages it
     is important to ex explore <,> yourself
     (S1A-003 103–106 FACE)

The retrospective, self-monitoring function can be signalled explicitly by the collocation with *I mean:*

(4) A: Well Xepe seems to love this idea of having a picnic but I'm not too sure about this
     B: Not if you've had lunch
     A: Because I'll have eaten anyway
     <u>Well I mean</u> part part of the reason I am eating will be so that I we don't have a picnic
     (S1A-006 028–031 FACE)

Well is pronounced rapidly without a vowel suggesting the speaker's impatience or implying that the reason he does not want to go on a picnic should be obvious.

However, many other 'change' functions are found in the corpus suggesting that *well* can be used in a number of different ways depending on the words it is combined with. When *well* is embedded in the turn it can, for instance, be used to return to an earlier topic or to introduce an explanatory comment or clarification (Halliday and Hasan 1976). In the following example the change (to a different topic or to a conclusion) is marked by a cluster of different pragmatic markers including *well* which is hardly audible:

(5) C: But I mean if I need some help I could still come
     A: Yeah but I don't think there'll be formal tutorials you can ask specific questions on occasions but you know unfortunately we've got major commitments <,> and now's the opportunity we've allocated to deal with that <,> <u>OK well anyway I mean</u> you four are the people who've come so you deserve the reward for your diligence
     (S1B-015 021–026 CLASSROOM LESSON)

In (6) *well obviously I mean* marks a conclusion and a correction in the course of the ongoing discourse:

(6) A: Oh well uh <,> no neither
     <u>Well Well</u> money <u>obviously I mean</u>
     I never have any <,> but uh <,>
     No it's just a matter of getting
     (S1A-095 006–0011 TELEPHONE)

Well has a number of functions where it is closely associated with the speaker's monitoring of the conversation. I have distinguished between the frame (*well* as a turn-taking device) and the transitional function.

2.8.2 *Well* as a turn-taking device

Well can draw attention to something new in the discourse. This can be a new turn but also a description, an explanation, narrative, etc.[13] The use of *well* can be described in a dialogic perspective as in Schegloff's description of the turn-initial *uhm*:

> . . . participants sometimes begin a turn by producing an 'uhm' just after the possible completion of a prior turn, then pausing, and then producing a turn rather than just delaying their start until they are 'ready'. They may be understood to proceed in this fashion precisely in order first to show their understanding of the current state of the talk and their stance towards it (i.e. a prior state is over, it is an appropriate occasion for a next turn, I will produce one) . . . (Schegloff 1981: 81)

Well is a powerful projection device pointing forwards to the next turn or discourse unit. In the example below the speaker takes control in the conversation in order to develop a point. *Well* has a framing function. It frequently occurs at boundaries in the discourse, for example, at an opening of the conversation or before a longish description or narrative. Many examples with *well* in this function were followed by a pause:[14]

(7) B: So uhm So he's going to punch the details into a <unclear word> screen <,>
    A: <u>Well</u> <,,> if there's anything if there's anything in one of the letters that I think is vaguely chatty I'm obviously David I'm not going to give him any of the personal stuff am I <,,>
    B: Or do whatever he needs to do
    (S1A-092 321–324 FACE)

The speaker uses *well* to signal a new turn, topic, an elaborate answer or clarification, etc.

However even when there were no pauses or other hesitation signals *well* can be analysed as a turn-taking device. This is particularly the case if it projects more than a single utterance or if it is accompanied by a 'preface' such as (*well let me address that*) (cf. Section 2.12.1). In the example below (from a conversation) *well* is used before a 'narrative answer' (the answer to a question asking for an extended answer in the form of a description or a narrative). Speaker A starts with a question about how B (and C) got involved in the Mike Heafy project (a dance project with both abled and disabled participants). B takes the turn first to elaborate on how she became interested in the project.

(8) A: Can you tell me how did you both get involved in the Mike Heafy project <,,>
    B: Shall I go first
    C: Yes
    B: <u>Well</u> I got involved through Celeste who <,> I used to dance with with London Contemporary <,> going back <,> twenty years or so
    (S1A-002 001–004 FACE)

Well is pronounced with a full vowel and a fall tone suggesting that *well* is used to introduce an extensive portion of the discourse.

Both pronunciation and prosodic features such as pauses are important to analyse *well* in this function. However, the criterion I have used for *well* in the turn-initiating function is that the contribution to the discussion continues over several utterances rather than prosody. The turn-taking function needs to be distinguished from *well* as a feedback signal to a question. *Well* as a feedback signal is, for instance, typically found in the answer to a question but also in other examples signalled by a rapid pronunciation using the reduced form of *well*. See Section 2.9.3 (*Well* as a feedback to questions).

2.8.3 Transition according to an agenda

Well also has transitional functions associated with its use as a contextualisation cue. It signals a change of topic or speech act according to an agenda or an 'interpretative frame', that is, the use of *well* can be explained with regard to background knowledge about the activity. The following example is from the face-to-face conversation sample but is untypical in that the conversation takes place at a university health centre between a doctor and his patient. Speaker A is a young (male) medical graduate and speaker B is an elderly housewife. B has complained earlier about suffering from glandular fever. *Well* has to be interpreted against the background of the shared knowledge of societal and communal norms and conventions. The doctor's question can be understood as a 'request to follow a procedure' (Levinson 1983: 386). The answer follows the agenda for doctor–patient communication (the doctor is in control of the conversation and asks questions about the patient's health, which the patient is supposed to answer).

(9) A: and d'you have a reasonable diet d'you think
     B: <u>Well</u> I eat one good cooked meal a day of meat and vegetables
     (S1A-051 031– 032 FACE)

Such examples have been little discussed (probably because they are not typical of conversation but of structured events where *well* has the function to mark transitions between stages in the event). Lam (2006: 102), however, found 'seemingly direct and non-abrasive answers' in her data from talk shows which she associated with 'considerative' aspects of *well*. In example (10) with the same speakers as in (9), *well* occurs both in the question (to mark a transition to a doctor-patient question-answer sequence) and in the answer reflecting the speakers' awareness of their roles as doctor and patient and their knowledge of the 'serious' use of questions and answers in the interview.

(10) A: A sore throat
     <u>Well</u> how old were you when the tonsils were taken out
     B: <u>Well</u> I had them taken out <,> in January
     A: This year
     B: Yeah
     (S1A-051 124–128 FACE)

Well is latched on to the preceding turn in B's answer and pronounced with reduced vowel. The doctor's *well* is more prominent (pronounced with full vowel).

According to Blakemore, the answer from the patient in such examples is 'an earnest one, designed to do the question justice' (Blakemore 2002: 136). The earnestness noticed by Blakemore can be regarded as an effect of the hesitation or 'stalling' meaning of *well* associated with word-search. We can make comparisons with other answers to questions preceded by *well* (especially in conversation) where the answerer makes light of the question by sidestepping the information which he or she is expected to give in reply to the question. (Cf. Section 2.9.3 on answers to questions.)

Compare also Bolinger's (1989: 312) suggestion that the speaker acts according to a protocol if *well* is present:

> Or take a receptionist who greets a party in an anteroom with
> How can I help you?
> This is or pretends to be spontaneous, an offer from the heart. But if the same receptionist asks
> Well, how can I help you?
> we sense something like 'How can I help you, given the need to tie this in somehow with the business of this office?' It is an action in accord with a protocol.

The absence of a pragmatic marker in such examples would be 'an absence with meaning' and a potential source of interactional trouble as has been pointed out with regard to classroom discourse (Dorr-Bremme 1990: 389). For example, students in the classroom might react as if the absence of a pragmatic marker meant 'I (the teacher) have nothing on my agenda now' (ibid. 389). I will return to similar examples when I discuss *well* in different text types (e.g. *well* in broadcast discussion; see Section 2.12.1).

2.8.4 Transition to a quotation

Well (and other pragmatic markers) can introduce or 'frame' a quotation. In such cases *well* typically collocates with a form of *say* or *think* (in particular *said well*) and occasionally other verbs (*wonder, ask*). Although *well* (or another pragmatic marker) is never obligatory before direct speech, it makes the description more vivid and emotional. *Well* is part of the staging of a little dialogue and conveys an 'affective report' (Haviland 1989) of the protagonist's words and adds to the vividness of the description by presenting what took place as happening before our eyes. Another frequent collocation is with filled or unfilled pauses (before *well*) suggesting that *well* has a boundary function.

(11) And I said oh really <,>
      And uhm and he said <,>well what do you think Jenny
      And I thought oh God
      And I said <,> well I couldn't say no you're not boring because it was so obvious
      (S1A-091 0075–0078 TELEPHONE)

Well introducing direct speech was also frequent together with other pragmatic markers or interjections (*well fuck off, oh well, well look, well you know, well yes, oh well you know,* a tag question) which suggests that *well* does more than signal the transition to direct speech. *Well* co-occurs with the change to a 'quoting voice' in which the speaker re-enacts a previous speech situation.

The function of *well* to introduce a quotation is characteristic of certain text types (mainly conversation) where speakers tell stories in order to be entertaining and keep the hearer's interest. It was more frequent in telephone conversation than in informal conversation (cf. Section 2.11.2).

2.9 *Well* and involvement

Involvement is 'concerned with how to express or not to express feelings, attitudes and prejudices' (Östman 1995: 104). *Well* in this function is more than a turn-taking device. It marks the speaker's involvement with the hearer, co-operation and interest in what is going on in the discourse.

Well signals that the speaker has considered whether what has just been said is good or bad, whether the information in the preceding text is sufficient, whether it meets expectations before taking a stance by either agreeing or disagreeing with the previous speaker or by expressing an opinion on what has been said. A distinction can be made between examples where *well* expresses an attitude or modifies a previous assertion and where it reacts to a question.

The following subcategories of involvement are distinguished:

- agreement
- disagreement
- evaluation (something is good or bad)
- feedback to a preceding question

Additional sub-senses can be indicated by collocations: *well at least* (extenuation),[15] *well yes* (qualified agreement), *well no* (qualified disagreement), *well but* (softened disagreement), *well . . . but* (partial agreement), *well anyway* (resigned acceptance).

Involvement categories are slippery since the attitudes also depend on how the speaker wants to present him- or herself and on the type of social activity. Moreover, much of the interpretation depends on the prosody and, we can hypothesise, on body language. Not surprisingly *well* has been described as a 'gestural' interjection indicating a relationship between a mental state or attitude and 'a vocal "portrayal" of that state' (Schourup 2001: 1050) (cf. Section 2.2).

2.9.1 *Well* and agreement

When *well* has the meaning agreement it can for instance introduce innocent remarks; it is used 'phatically' to signal that the speaker attends to what is said without necessarily agreeing or disagreeing. Speaker B is describing how the French prepare coffee:

(12) B: They had a tendency to cook their coffee in saucepans <,>
      Make their coffee I should say in saucepans

A: <u>Well</u> they bring it to the boil and whip it off the stove
B: Mm something like that
(S1A-009 182–185 FACE)

The function of *well* to express agreement has been described as empathetic (Green 2006) or harmonising (de Klerk 2005). *Well* avoids overt disagreement and emphasises the close bond between speaker and hearer.

According to Haviland (1989: 45), agreement is a complex category: 'Here is part of the complexity of agreement: it is possible to express a reservation by agreeing with only part of, or something conditional on an utterance – an oppositional move in the garb of the agreement'.

Well can for instance be used for agreement with some reservation. In the following example husband (A) and wife (B) are discussing what is happening to their wallflowers:

(13) B: What so all the flowers have died on them
     A: <u>Well</u> these other ones are not coming along very well so
     B: The ones on the right hand side you can just cut the tops off and leave them
     (S1A-007 002–005 FACE)

A does not disagree with B but points out that what is said 'is not exactly new information' (Svartvik 1980: 173). The meaning of reservation or resignation is also indicated by the pronunciation (drawling and with a full vowel).

In (14) (with the same speakers) *well* also expresses the speaker's attitude. Speaker A has given away a glazed sash window which he now thinks he could have grown seeds on so that he would not have to buy plants. C is the daughter in the family:

(14) B: No you can't blame her for that really can you
     C: If you gave it to her Dad
     B: No
     A: <u>Well</u> these damn plants have shot up in price so much over the last year or two
     B: Yes
     (S1A-007 018–021 FACE)

Well is pronounced loudly and with a full vowel indicating the speaker's despair or irritation.

As suggested by examples (13) and (14), *well* can have emotional connotations when it expresses agreement (or disagreement). Speakers can also make explicit their emotions, that is, the emotional meaning is conventionalised. Emotion is always present in combinations such as *oh well, ah well* and *right well*. According to Bolinger, '*ah well* and *oh well* are stereotyped for resignation' (1989: 324). This is also supported by intonation. In the following example *ah well* indicates indifference or the speaker's resigned acceptance of the fact that the botanical garden the speaker and hearer want to visit is probably busy on Sundays. *Ah well* is uttered with an exaggerated intonation with drawling of the vowel in *ah* and falling tone on *well*:

(15) B: I bet it's busy on Sundays <,>
     A: Probably is

     B: <u>Ah well</u>
     A: It's pretty hard to park there anyway No
     (S1A-006 255–259 FACE)

Other usages where *well* has emotional meaning are less frequent. *Well that's fair enough (then)* expresses concession and *well that's all right* resignation:

(16) B: Oh you did
       A: Because we otherwise we would've been overdrawn and then I would've been out of pocket
       B: <u>Oh well Right that's fair enough</u> then
       (S1A-005 214–218 FACE)

In (17) *well that's all right* signals the speaker's reluctant acceptance:

(17) C: When I'm qualified as far as I can tell <,> I'm going to get uhm to do lots and lots of photocopying and funny things like that <unclear-words>
       A: Uhm
       A: <u>Well that's all right</u> you're in good company I mean you with your Oxford degree are now going to be photocopying and Sue with her degree is actually putting things in alphabetical order that should make you both feel a lot better
       (S1A-011 026–031 FACE)

The emotions expressed are more commonly negative than positive which suggests that *well* is more frequent when something does not go the speaker's way (i.e. it is associated with disagreement rather than agreement). *Well* is allied with 'reluctance, regret, resignation or indifference, sometimes impatience, irritation, embarrassment, or defensiveness; sometimes caution, uncertainty, doubt or fear' (Carlson 1984: 43). Carlson only looked at conversation (dialogue in detective fiction). In other text types (such as a heated discussion) the emotional character of *well* might be even more striking.

Some meanings of *well* are infrequent in the corpus and are less conventionalised, especially as they are dependent on the immediate context. *Well* can, for instance, be used in exclamations of surprise, that is, a clearly attitudinal meaning. In the following example *well* is emotional as seen by the collocation (*what the hell*). A and B are young female students. A has ordered a photo of Woodville Feast. She is surprised when she finds out that B did not buy a photo.

(18) B: D'you order a ball photo <,,>
       A: Ball photo
       B: Not ball Woodville Feast
       A: Yeah Unframed
       B:
       A: But crested
       B: Oh that's nice
       A: <u>Well what the hell</u> <eh> you didn't
       (S1A-039 202–212 FACE)

2.9.2 *Well* and disagreement

It is typical of *well* that it is used both when 'everything is as it should be' and when something has not taken place according to expectations.

Disagreement (denial, correcting an error, rejection, criticism) is expressed in the following example:

> (19) B: Oh quite yes
> C: No it's the it's the wrong side anyway
> A: <u>Well</u> it's not that far away
> B: Yes I think it is
> (S1A-011 069–072 FACE)

In (20), the combination with *anyway* (later in the utterance) suggests that the disagreement is qualified. *Well* is pronounced rapidly with reduced vowel. The speakers are discussing what film they want to see on the video:

> (20) B: Well we're going to have endless discussions about what film to get out aren't we Can you set it up on your <,> uhm uhm sort of stereo thingummybob that you
> A: So you're stuck with it aren't you <u>Well</u> it's all set up <u>anyway</u>
> The only thing is if uh <,,> arty Because it's going to be an arty film almost certainly because you like arty films <,> and Xepe likes arty films
> (S1A-006 080–084 FACE)

2.9.3 *Well* as a feedback to questions

According to Svartvik (1980: 174) 'there seems to be no reason to treat *well* prefixed to answers as a special category since the same qualifying function obtains in answers and non-answers alike'. *Well* in the answer to a question can have several functions. However, the frequency of *well* to signal an insufficient answer may motivate treating it as a special sub-sense of *well*. 'Insufficient answers' have been the object of much discussion since they are often introduced by *well* (originally pointed out by Robin Lakoff 1973). Lakoff discussed answers to questions where the speaker used *well* to mark that the answer was inappropriate in some way, for example, because the answer does not give the information sought. This would explain, for instance, why it would be unacceptable to use *well* in the answer to a direct question as in:

> A: What time is it?
> B: Well three o'clock.

The answerer's 'it's three o'clock' will be accepted provided only that it is three o'clock' (Lakoff 1973: 456). According to Lakoff (1973: 458), 'it seems that *well* is used in case the respondent knows he is not giving directly the information the questioner sought'. In (21) *well* (pronounced with a lengthened vowel) is used to signal an insufficient or indirect answer for which the speaker does not take responsibility. The answer is not appropriate since the speaker does not provide the information about where he is looking ('I'm just looking'):

(21) A: Where else do you look John
B: <u>Well</u> uhm just looking
That's really kind of uh quite specific really cos they have a certain sort of job and that
A: That's your main source
(S1A-34 220–224 FACE)

The answer in the following example is also insufficient since the answerer does not use one of the options provided by the question to provide the information. The speaker pauses before saying that it was 'sort of nice' making it possible for the hearer to deduce that the place the speaker went was not what one could expect. *Well*, which is pronounced with a full vowel, adds some dramatic effect to the answer (which is accompanied by laughter):

(22) A: Uhm<,> Did you go somewhere nice <,>
B: <u>Well</u> <,> it was sort of nice <laugh> there
(S1A-018 012–014 FACE)

Well is also needed in answers clarifying or explaining something which has been overlooked. In the conversation below between two young women, B is not satisfied with A's answer that the park is very big and asks a 'continuation question' requesting clarification:

(23) A: It's a huge great expanse of green you know <unclear words>
It's very it's very big
I mean it's not like a
B: I mean is there much on it
Is it just green like just like a park
A: I see
Well it's very hilly I mean lots of little
B: Ah
(S1A-006 239–247 FACE)

In the following example, speaker B has not provided all the information that A wanted. He has said that he 'toured the Voronezh' but not how long he stayed. He therefore provides a clarification.

(24) B: I haven't been to the Black Sea but I have toured the Voronezh
A: How long did you stay there<,>
B: <u>Well</u> I had a month's study tour and then three months' exchange <,,>
(S1A-014 078–080 FACE)

Speaker B uses the clipped version of *well* indicating that he provides the extra information but that he does not want to give a longish description of what he did on his holiday.

2.10 *Well* and politeness

In addition to the constraints imposed by coherence and involvement we need to consider the role of politeness. *Politeness* is 'concerned with the interactional constraints we follow when establishing, maintaining or breaking interpersonal relationships' (Östman 1995: 104). In the analysis of *well* politeness is associated with hedging.

The motive for *well* may be to soften a potentially face-threatening act or to reinforce it (e.g. in an argument). However, in both cases something must be added to *well* to show how it is intended. Combinations such as *well I don't know*, *well I think*, *well perhaps*, *well maybe* and *well you know* occur and have the function of mitigating illocutionary force in contexts which can be experienced as face-threatening. In (25) a previous speaker has been telling the others how she found a fly in the sardines. Speaker A continues on the same topic by telling the others how she discovered ants, which had been in the salt cellar, in her food.

> (25) D: You're lucky the salt was flowing in my opinion
> Fancy complaining about ants being in it
> A: <u>Well maybe</u> they put them in instead of rice
> (S1A-055 253–255 FACE)

Well is reinforcing and as a result assertive and authoritative in contexts where it co-occurs with *certainly, surely, actually, really, as I say, unquestionably*, etc. This function can be distinguished from *well* expressing disagreement since it does not involve an 'error' or misunderstanding but illocutionary force. In the following example, both *well* and *the thing was* are used to reinforce the speaker's point. Speaker B has organised an event where everyone has paid a quid, the point being that they were going to have strawberries and cream.

> (26) A: Oh well
> Right
> Well right that's fair enough then
> B: <u>Well the thing was that the whole point</u>
> <u>was that</u> we were going to have strawberries
> and cream
> (S1A-005 216–219)

The pronunciation of *well* with a full vowel, pronounced clearly and loudly further underlines the assertiveness with which the speaker makes her point.

To summarise, I have tried to give a more abstract and formal description of the meaning potential of *well* by distinguishing certain parameters along which different sub-senses of *well* can be organised. A number of functional categories have been distinguished subsumed under coherence, involvement or politeness (see Table 2.2).

Well has a large number of different functions in the corpus. We can assume that particular functions become conventionalised as a result of recurrence. As a result, a number of sub-senses could be distinguished on the basis of their frequencies and salience, in particular, in conversation. Other sub-senses were less conventionalised and depended more

Table 2.2 The functions of *well* in informal conversation

Coherence
word search and self-repair
transition to a new turn
transition according to an agenda
transition to a quotation
Involvement
agreeing
disagreeing
feedback to a preceding question
Politeness

on collocations. In addition, there are connotations or effects which are closely associated with other functions or with the wider context. It was for instance typical of many uses of *well* that they expressed the speaker's emotions.

However, meaning potentials should also account for specialised or innovative uses in different text types. This is the topic of Sections 2.11–2.14.

2.11 *Well* in private dialogue

A distinction is made between *well* in face-to-face conversation and in telephone conversation.

2.11.1 *Well* in face-to-face conversation

Face-to-face conversation represents a basic human activity characterised by the aim of the speakers to establish and maintain a close relationship. At the outset, we notice that *well* was frequent in face-to-face conversation although not as frequent as in telephone conversation (cf. Section 2.3). It is also more frequent than other markers such as *you know* and *I mean* (Biber et al. 1999: 1096; cf Chapter 2). It occurs together with other markers such as *oh* or *alright* but not with structural markers (discourse markers) such as *and, meanwhile* and *now* in conversations among friends (Redeker 1990).[16] In the ICE-GB, a sample of 200 words representing face-to-face conversation has been analysed in detail (cf. Section 2.3). *Well* occurred with a filled pause *(uh(m))* in 18 examples, 15 examples of which were found in initial position. Other typical collocates in my conversation data were *yeah/yes* (13 examples), *no* (7 examples), *I think* (7 examples), *I mean* (6 examples), *right* (2 examples), *I suppose, oh* (8 examples), *ah, I don't know, you know* (4 examples), *as I say,* and *now. Well* was also frequent in clusters (hesitation strings) such as *yeah no no well yeah, oh right oh well.* 'Stacked' pragmatic markers were both embedded in the turn (example 27) and turn-initial (example 28):

(27) A: I'm sure it would <,,>
       I think you uh
       Well I don't know

> I think I always feel I'd like
> to get away from the place for a bit
> (S1A-095 280–283 FACE)

The example illustrates the use of *well I don't know* to fill a pause followed by self-correction.

In (28) *well* is not only a turn-taking device but 'holds the floor' while the speaker thinks of what to say:

(28)   B: You mean a novel
       A: Yes yes
       C: <u>Well uh uh uh</u> no there's pleasure in any sort of book isn't there yeah a
       textbook
       (S1A-013 123–126 FACE)

Well occurs in different positions in face-to-face conversation although the initial position 'could generally be regarded as the natural one' (de Klerk 2005: 1190; cf. Section 2.4). The position of *well* (in conversation) is briefly mentioned by Svartvik (1980: 169) who found that '*well* occurred with equal frequency at the beginning of a new turn, *ie* after speaker switch, and embedded in a single speaker's utterance.' My figures for initial position in conversation are even larger. 124 examples out of 200 were turn-initial (62%). In addition, there were 23 examples where *well* was preceded by *uh(m)*, *yes*, *yeah*, *mm*, *oh god* or *right* (11.5%). My figures are also larger than those given by de Klerk in her study of Xhosa English. Compare de Klerk (2005: 1190): 'Of further interest is the fact that of all occurrences of *well*, 32.4% [158] were turn-initial (in a further 48 cases, *ja*, *um* and *okay* preceded *well*).[17] The position of *well* may serve as a cue to its function. When *well* was embedded in the turn it always had a coherence function (word-search, self-repair). Initial position, on the other hand, was associated with involvement. Moreover, when *well* was used as a turn-taking device establishing coherence by pointing backwards and forwards in the discourse it was always initial (see Table 2.3).

Questions and answers are unusual in face-to-face conversation compared with other

Table 2.3 *Well* in different positions in the turn in face-to-face conversation

Position	Number	Per cent
Initial[18]	124	62%
Initial (after a preceding *yes*, *yeah*, *uh(m)*, *right*, *oh*, *OK* or a combination of these)	23	11.5%
Medial	53	26.5%
Total	200	100%

text types such as interviews or courtroom examinations. The conversation consists mainly of what Innes (2010) refers to as 'topic talk' rather than of question-answer pairs (as in an interview) or talk on a pre-fixed topic as in a broadcast discussion where questions are used mainly by the speaker in power to control the discourse. In the conversational data *well* occurred in the answer to questions in 34 examples (out of 200), slightly more often after a yes-no question (16 examples) than after a *wh*-question (14 examples).[19] *Well* occurred most frequently in declarative sentences (see Table 2.4).

Table 2.4 *Well* in different clause-types (only clause- initial examples of *well* are counted)

Context	Number	Per cent
Declarative*	137	93.2%
Interrogative	6	4.1%
Imperative	4	2.7%
Total	147	100%

* Including elliptical examples such as *well yes*

Well is interpreted differently in interrogative sentences, statements and imperatives depending on the text type. *Well* in interrogatives is for instance mainly mitigating in face-to-face conversation and challenging in other text types such as court examination (cf. Section 2.3).

The prosodic features I have looked at are pauses and pronunciation (the distinction between a full and reduced pronunciation).

Well was separated from the rest of the utterance by a short or long pause that followed it indicating 'comma intonation' in 7 out of 200 examples. It was preceded by a pause in roughly the same number of examples (see Table 2.5).

Table 2.5 *Well* and pauses in face-to-face conversation

Type of pause	Number	Per cent
Pause before *well*	7	3.5%
Pause after *well*	5	2.5%
Long pause before, short after	1	0.5%
No pause	187	93.5%
Total	200	100%

We also need to consider the co-occurrence with filled pauses (*uh(m)*, *yeah*, *yes*). *Well* co-occurred with a filled pause with *uh(m)* in 20 examples (in 15 examples before *well*) and in 12 examples with *yeah* or *yes* (7/12 examples before *well*). Some other frequent collocations were *oh well* (9 examples), *well I think* (7 examples), *well I mean* (6 examples), *well you know* (or *you know well*) (4 examples), *right well* (or *well right*) (3 examples).

Well was pronounced with a full vowel in 64.3% of the examples (108/168)[20] (see Table 2.6).

Table 2.6 Pronunciation of *well* in face-to-face conversation

Pronunciation	Number	Per cent
Full	108	54%
Reduced	60	30%
Unclear	32	16%
Total	200	100%

Schourup (1985: 85) correlates the full pronunciation with the use of *well* as a pause (*well* used for word-search or self-repair). He also found that *well* in the reduced form was used in some answers to questions (e.g. those where the question had been wrongly answered).

The functions of *well* are shown in Table 2.7:

Table 2.7 The functions of *well* in face-to-face conversation

Function	Number
Coherence	
Transition to a new turn	9
Transition according to an agenda	–
Direct speech	10
Word-search	3
Self-repair	29
Involvement	
Agreement	68
Disagreement	36
Insufficient answers	33
Politeness	12
Total	200

Well was infrequent as a coherence device introducing a new turn or description (9 examples). It was used for agreement including conclusion, hesitant agreement *(well then)*, disagreement (denial, rejection, correction of a misunderstandings) as well as quali-fied disagreement (extenuation *well at least,* dismissal *well anyway)*. *Well* in answers to questions expresses the speaker's unwillingness or inability to answer the question, but also clarification or explanation (33 examples in all). It was found in 10 examples intro-ducing direct speech. Speakers strive to be entertaining, witty, conspicuous and take the opportunity to describe in a dramatic way what has happened to them or to someone else. Compare also telephone conversation where these uses are even more frequent (Section 2.3).

Well was also used for hedging (with collocates such as *I think, I suppose, probably)* associated with illocutionary force and politeness or (with collocates such as *the thing is, certainly, as I say*) to reinforce what is said (12 examples).

Table 2.8 shows that *well* in informal conversation is used for involvement rather than for coherence.

Table 2.8 *Well* in coherence, involvement and politeness functions in face-to-face conversation

Function	Number	Per cent
Coherence	51	25.5%
Involvement	137	68.5%
Politeness	12	6%
Total	200	100%

There was some correlation between pronunciation and function. In my data the full form was used for pausing and repair as in Schourup's study referred to above. It was also frequent in the disagreement function. The reduced form was more frequent before direct speech (see Table 2.9).

Table 2.9 The pronunciation of *well* in different functions in conversation

	Reduced	Full vowel	Total
Coherence			
Transition to a new turn	3	4	7
Transition according to an agenda	–	–	–
Direct speech	6	3	9
Word-search	–	3	3
Self-repair	5	20	25
Involvement			
Agreement	21	36	57
Disagreement	5	22	27
Insufficient answers	16	15	31
Politeness	4	5	9

The functions of *well* are closely associated with who the speakers are. The speakers in the face-to-face conversations are family, friends or acquaintances and they engage in talk 'as a human duty' (Mey [1993] 2001: 136). They use *well* because it is a 'friendly' pragmatic marker with the function of cementing social relationships and creating solidarity within the group. The presence of *well* makes the force of the utterance 'almost placatory and less abrasive by showing that it has been given due consideration' (de Klerk 2005: 1195). On the other hand, *well* is not authoritative or challenging, which are functions associated with court debates or legal cross-examinations. It follows that *well* in conversation has a conflict-avoiding function. If there is disagreement it is mild (resulting in clarification or correction) and it does not affect the social relationship between the speakers. In the following example the conversation takes place in the participants' home (C is a student who has to fill in a form about how many people are living in the property; A and B are husband and wife). C uses the full form of *well*, which is emphatic (turn 7) or corrective (turn 9).

(29) 1 A: Is it I don't remember that
2 B: <u>Well</u> she says she has to <u>anyway</u> because it's in the form she gets <u>anyway</u>
3 A: <u>Well</u> she <u>probably</u> has to put the number of people occupying the whole property <,> <u>presumably</u>
4 B: <u>Well I don't suppose</u> she knows how many people are living in the whole property
5 C: Me
6 B: Mhm
7 C: <u>Well at least</u> ten or twenty people
8 B: <u>Well</u> that's <u>a bit of</u> a difference <,,>
9 C: <u>Well</u> there are ten flats
(S1A-007 240–249 FACE)

An observation we can make about *well* is that it is hardly ever 'neutral' but usually expresses different stances (emotions and attitudes) associated with agreement or disagreement. In the following example speaker A has thrown away a window frame and now regrets it since it could have been used to cover her box of seeds.

(30) 1 B: I tell you what I could look out for and that's a picture frame <,> because that's got a glass in it hasn't it Wouldn't be very large but it'd be big enough to go over a box of seeds
      2 C: or a clip frame those are quite cheap
      3 A: <u>Well</u> I I I want something bigger than one box of seeds
      4 No That damn thing would've done ideally <u>well</u> it annoys me to see it there sitting smugly growing her seeds
      5 B: <u>Well</u> does she use it
      6 C: <u>Well</u> she's using it
      7 B: <u>Well</u> you can't blame her lovey
(S1A-007 062–071 FACE)

'Well she's using it' expresses the speaker's reluctant agreement to what has just been said. It is followed by B's reproachful 'well you can't blame her'. Notice also 'well it annoys me'. The appearance of *well* in the question 'Well does she use it' is prompted by the insufficiency of what speaker A has just said and emphasises that speaker B wants an answer.

To sum up, speakers use *well* with a large number of different functions in face-to-face conversation. As we have seen, the coherence function was not typical of *well*. When we look at its core functions we see that it was typically used for involvement or stance.

That *well* has a rich meaning potential is illustrated by its multifunctionality, in particular, its uses in conversation to convey a certain attitude. *Well* was above all a signal that 'everything is at it should be' (the agreeing function). If there was disagreement it was mild (qualified or partial). *Well* was also used as a mitigator associated with illocutionary force. It has been shown that its meaning potential can be exploited to meet the demands of informal conversation, for example, the need to maintain harmonious relationships and avoid disagreement, to be interesting, to show one's feelings and reactions, etc. As a result, *well* in conversation is above all a friendly marker although it can have other functions as well. Moreover, its core functions (sub-senses) could be overshadowed by emotional connotations such as resignation or reluctance. The use of *well* to introduce direct speech can be explained not only in terms of its coherence function but above all as a resource in conversation to arouse the hearer's interest. Speakers do not want to be bores; they tell stories and anecdotes using *well* with direct speech to catch the hearer's interest. Principles having to do with politeness and involvement ('consider the hearer') can be assumed to be as important and contribute as much to co-operation in conversation as the well-known Gricean maxims.

When the speaker selects *well* he or she also makes a choice with regard to prosody (pauses, intonation, pronunciation) and position in the utterance or turn and on the basis of what has come before in the context. *Well* was used in declarative sentences rather than in question-answer dialogues. It was mostly used in initial position. The formal properties function as cues. They are however associated with the functional potential of *well* in ways which are complex since they involve frequencies. Prosodically *well* occurred, for example, both with a full vowel and with a reduced pronunciation.

2.11.2 *Well* in telephone conversation

Both face-to-face and telephone conversation are highly interactive but the conditions for the interaction are different since the speakers cannot see each other on the telephone. This may explain why *well* is needed more often in telephone conversations than in face-to-face conversation (and other text types). Moreover, unlike face-to-face conversation the participants normally have special roles as caller and answerer associated with special tasks.

I will first consider formal properties such as the position of *well* in telephone conversation. *Well* was found in initial position in the turn in 85 examples (42.5%) and in addition in 53 examples preceded by *yes, yeah, uh(m), right, oh* or clusters of these (26.5%). A comparison with informal conversation shows that *well* was more frequent with another marker in initial position in telephone conversation. 31% of the examples were embedded in the speaker turn which is similar to the situation in conversation (see Table 2.10).

Table 2.10 *Well* in different positions in telephone conversation

Position	Number	Per cent
Initial*	85	42.5%
Initial after a preceding *yes, yeah, uh(m), right, oh,* *OK* or a combination of these	53	26.5%
Medial	57	28.5%
Final	5	2.5%
Total	200	100%

* Including examples where *well* (with or without a preceding marker) is not followed by a clause

As in face-to-face conversation, *well* occurred above all in declarative sentences (66% in face-to-face conversation vs 67% in telephone conversation) (see Table 2.11). There were 32 examples of *well* introducing answers in question-answer exchanges in telephone calls which is similar to the frequency of *well* in answers in face-to-face conversation and suggests that the reason for the call is 'topic talk' or chatting.

Table 2.11 *Well* in different clause-types in telephone conversation (only clause- initial examples of *well* are counted)

Context	Number	Per cent
Declarative *	131	91.6%
Interrogative	10	7%
Imperative	2	1.4%
Total	143	100%

* Including elliptical examples such as *well yes*

Well was more frequent with pauses than in face-to-face conversation (see Table 2.12).

Table 2.12 *Well* and pauses in telephone conversation

Type of pause	Number	Per cent
Pause before *well*	18	9%
Pause after *well*	7	3.5%
Pause before and after *well*	1	0.5%
No pause	174	87%
Total	200	100%

Well was preceded by pauses in 9% of the examples to be compared with 3.5% in face-to-face conversation (see Section 2.11.1). *Well* was also frequent with filled pauses (*uh (m)* 21 examples; *yeah* 25 examples). Other frequent collocations were *oh well* (9 examples*), I mean* (8 examples), *you know* (6 examples) and *I don't know* (5 examples).

Moreover, *well* in telephone conversation frequently co-occurred with *OK* (4 examples) and *right* (4 examples).

The functions of *well* in telephone conversation are shown in Table 2.13:

Table 2.13 *Well* in different functions in telephone conversation

Function	Number
Coherence	
Transition to a new turn	2
Transition according to an agenda	14
Direct speech	14
Word search	15
Self-repair	37
Involvement	
Agreeing	44
Disagreeing	34
Insufficient answers	37
Politeness	3
Total	200

The distribution over major categories is shown in Table 2.14.

Table 2.14 The distribution of *well* over the major functions coherence, involvement and politeness in telephone conversation

Function	Number	Per cent
Coherence	82	41%
Involvement	115	57.5%
Politeness	3	1.5%
Total	200	100%

We can expect coherence and interpersonal relations to vary in frequency depending on features of the text type. What makes telephone conversation special is that the speakers cannot see each other which makes turn-taking more difficult. Moreover, speakers have roles as caller and answerer.

In telephone conversation *well* can be extended to functions which are needed to meet the special demands of this medium. *Well* as a coherence device includes examples where speakers use *well* (together with other pragmatic markers such as *yes, yeah, uhm*, etc.) as a floor-holding signal to show that they are 'still there'. The examples have been classified as word-search (cf. 'delay' or 'staller'). As indicated by the frequent occurrence of this function in telephone conversation we can assume that *well* compensates for the absence of face-to-face contact. In other types of discourse this use of *well* with other markers might make the speaker seem disorganised or hesitant.

> (31) A: Yes
>   She's got to have strength
>   So we all told her that but <,>
>   And I'm frightened to ask her in case it you know
>   I'll wait
>   I'll bring it up when she's on her own
>   I'll bring it up when she's on her own
>   B: <u>Yes Well Uhm</u> She said to me uhm uh the other day that she
>   wasn't eating very much and that the doctors had said not to
>   encourage her to
>   (S1A-094 120-130 TELEPHONE)

Speaker A and B are talking about a common friend whose mother has had an operation. Speaker A does not want to bring up the topic unless her friend is on her own. The core function of *well* is delay or hesitation. However, on the telephone the combined markers have the additional function to show that the speaker is still present on the line. The meaning is selected or evoked because it is useful in the telephone conversation. *Well* is prototypically used when the speaker searches for words but can also fulfil the needs of the participants in the telephone conversation to signal their presence and involvement in the conversation.

Well in final position (5 examples) is also primarily floor-holding 'carrying the strong implication that something will follow' (Schourup 1985: 91):

> (32) B: But uh <,> and I just smiled about
>   something and you know <,> <u>well</u>
>   A: That's it
>   (S1A-092 070–71 TELEPHONE)

Well was also frequently used in what I have referred to as self-repairs coinciding with a coherence break in the middle of the turn. These represent a broad category which can be subsumed under what Schiffrin (1987: 125) refers to as 'reflexive frame breaks': 'speakers treat their own just-completed discourse as talk open to their own evaluation, displacing it as if it were already prior experience available for reflection and commentary'. Speakers use *well*s for example for elaboration or clarification, asides, self-repair, self-posed questions, etc. (cf. Section 2.8.1).

In the following example, the speaker anticipates that the hearer will need clarification of what has been said (*well I think I mean*):

(33) B: Yeah
       A: And as I say Richards has been quite
       negative and they <,> cut off all the
       scoring shots
       <u>Well I think</u> they
       <u>I mean</u> they
       I think they did pretty well to get
       to <,> end up like that
       (S1A-095 090–094 TELEPHONE)

Well is used together with self-interruption and repair:

(34) A: Have they gone now
       B: <u>There's uhm No Well yes No There's people here the there's no news I</u>
       <u>meant to say</u>
       A: Oh I see
       (S1A-091 158–168 TELEPHONE)

The speaker starts saying something, stops (marked by *uhm no well yes no*) and then resumes the conversational thread.

Well on the telephone is, however, mainly used to signal that the speaker wants to continue. In (35) the speaker stops in order to make an evaluation and signals the change with *well*:

(35) B: It went i incredibly well
       I mean I just thought I'll just
       wait for these bastards to ask me to
       read this because they gave it to me
       before you know
       <u>Well</u>
       And it was delightful
       (S1A-092 037–40 TELEPHONE)

There is a high frequency of *well* together with direct quotation. *Well* occurred 14 times and is even more frequent than in face-to-face conversation in this function. This reflects the fact that narratives (personal experiences or anecdotes) are a frequent feature of telephone conversation (and face-to-face conversation). As seen from the following example, the speaker's narrative is 'densely packed with presented utterances' (cf. Rühlemann 2007: 141) whose function is to hold the hearer's interest:

(36) <u>He said</u> he was a palm-reader
       and <u>he said</u> <u>he said uhm</u> well you're obviously <laugh> slow <,>
       and <laughter> <u>he said</u> you're obviously terribly

slow very imperceptive
and you've got an appalling memory <laughter>
My hackles are really rising by this time
And uhm and <u>he said</u> and if you
want to pass your exams you'd really
better start now
And I and <u>I said</u> oh yes and
uhm and <,> where did you uhm learn
to do this then palm-read
<u>He said</u> from a book
<u>I said well</u> you're obviously not very
good at it are you <,>
Yeah
And then <u>he said</u> uhm and then I
<u>said</u> I was going to aerobics
He and <u>he said</u> <laugh> why
<u>I said well</u> you know why not it's good for you
<u>He said</u> <,> <u>well</u> there's not really
very much point
you're going to get fat anyway
(S1A-091 029–045 TELEPHONE)

Said occurred 13 times, 4 times followed by *well*.

As in face-to-face conversation speakers use *well* mainly for agreement, that is, to express that everything is as it should be. In (37) *well* shows that the speaker has considered what to say against the background of the preceding discourse before taking up a stance to add something which has been overlooked. *Well* makes the speaker's contribution less abrupt than the corresponding utterance without *well*

(37) B: Uh zilch
      A: Yeah
      B: Yeah
      A: <u>Well</u> he had an absolute beast of a ball
      B: Really
      A: A sort of thrown–high bouncer fourth ball I think
      (S1A-095 045–050 TELEPHONE)

When *well* was potentially conflictive its negative effects could be shrugged off by laughter. B's husband (referred to as 'he') has not bought food for dinner because he had no carrier bag.

(38) A: Couldn't he hold it under his arm
      B: <u>Well</u> you would've thought so wouldn't you but <laugh>
      <laugh> Maybe he forgot and that's an excuse
      (S1A-093 255–258 TELEPHONE)

Well in telephone conversation is used for special transaction-management tasks which involve routinisation and co-operation between the participants. In the following example *right well* is used to suggest the end of a topic and the introduction of a new topic. Speaker B has had 'a horrible bank statement' but has sent a cheque that should be cleared (changed) soon. *Right well OK* concludes the topic in the preceding discourse. The second *well* introduces a new topic.

> (39) B: I put that cheque in <unclear-word> <unclear-word> <,>
> A: Should get changed on Friday so
> B: Uhm uhm
> A: <unclear-words> Uhm <,,>
> B: <u>Right Well OK Well</u> I'll try and get back a
> bit earlier <unclear-words>
> A: Well you know see how you go
> Don't worry about it
> (S1A-099 201–210 TELEPHONE)

In the example below *right right well (then)* is part of the negotiation to come to an agreement. Speaker B bumped into a girl who said she was writing for a magazine and therefore can get into a dance event which is planned. Speaker A uses *right well then* to signal that what follows is a conclusion. As in other examples extended meanings are often marked in addition by collocation:

> (40) B: She was a girl <,> I don't know who she was <,> I don't know
> I didn't get her name <,> She's coming down
> A: <u>Right Right well</u> she can get in for a quid <u>then</u> can't she
> B: Oh she said she could get in anyway so
> A: Right
> (S1A-100 126–134 TELEPHONE)

Well can also be a part of a little ritual with the function to mark the end of the telephone conversation. In the following example we understand A's *well (I'll see you later)* as an offer to close which is accepted by B (*yeah OK then*). *Well* occurs with special phrases such as *I'll see you later* (example 41), *I'll speak to you later* (42) or *thank you very much*. It is associated with agreement (acceptance) rather than disagreement. However, *well* has been analysed as transitional since the interpretation presupposes knowledge about how the telephone call is structured:

> (41) A: <u>All right then Well I'll see you later</u>
> B: Yeah OK then
> A: Bye
> B: Bye
> (S1A 219–221 TELEPHONE)

> (42) B: They're quite <,> you know
> Very nice guys

> B: Yeah they are definitely
> B: OK then
> A: OK
> B: <u>Well I'll speak to you later</u>
> A: Right speak to you then
> B: Cheers
> A: All right
> B: Bye
> A: Bye
> (S1A-100 296–304 TELEPHONE)

To summarise, *well* was frequent in telephone conversation even in comparison with face-to-face conversation. It was used more frequently for coherence functions which can be explained by the needs and demands imposed by speaking on the telephone. An important feature of the telephone conversation is, for instance, that turn-taking is more difficult since the speakers cannot see each other. *Well* is therefore used as a floor-holding device making it possible for the speaker to signal that he or she is still present on the line. This does not mean that *well* cannot be used to hold the floor in face-to-face conversation. However, in face-to-face conversation the speaker can also use other non-verbal signals to take the turn or to hold the floor.

We can also see more examples of *well* at topic boundaries and it is used in specific ways in the closing procedure of the telephone call. For example, in informal conversation I found no examples of *well* at topic boundaries. This difference can be explained by the fact that it is more difficult both to 'change gear' in the telephone conversation and to close the conversation. More co-operation is needed by the participants in the telephone conversation to agree to close and to perform the expected moves in the conversation.

There are also similarities between face-to-face and telephone conversation. Both in face-to-face and telephone conversation the 'harmonizing' function of *well* associated with agreement and hedging was important. *Well* in personal telephone calls was for instance used for agreement more often than for (a degree of) disagreement.

2.12 *Well* in public dialogue

We can expect differences in the use of *well* when we turn from private to public dialogue. Examples in this category are, for instance, broadcast discussions or interviews, parliamentary debates, legal cross-examinations and business transactions. *Well* was most frequent in business transactions followed by classroom lessons and interviews. The text types have in common that the interaction takes place in a professional setting and that the speakers have special roles and professional identities. The setting affects turn-taking, how the discourse is built up by questions and answers or by declarative sentences, etc. As we shall see, speakers can be expected to use *well* as a contextualisation cue to signal changes to a new stage of the activity. Moreover *well* is used in a number of new functions associated with the social situation.

2.12.1 *Well* in broadcast discussion

Discussions and debates have been less well described than conversation. A broadcast discussion needs to be understood in terms of the participation framework (e.g. the social identities of the participants) and the activity itself (how it is built up of smaller units each representing a special discourse task).The broadcast discussions providing the data here are furthermore unusual because of the presence of a moderator who is 'the pivotal person' (Levinson 1983: 371) and controls the turn-taking, length of the contributions and choice of topic. We can therefore expect differences in comparison with informal conversation where, as we have seen, speaker change occurs 'creatively' to use an expression by De Fina (1997: 339). The broadcast discussion can be taken to be more closely related to, for example, broadcast interviews, committee meetings and classroom discourse than to conversation because of the constraints on turn-taking.

The broadcast discussion has both dialogical and monological features since speakers are allowed to develop their ideas (their position or stance on a particular issue) at some length. The topics are disputable. that is, they are intended to provoke mutually exclusive positions. The moderator invites speakers to take the floor to discuss, for example, if women should be allowed as members of cricket clubs, the war in Iraq, footpath preservation, ghost writers, modern British composers, the honours list, the National Health Service. The discussion has two or more participants who are experts in the area discussed. In particular the broadcast discussion has an audience (those listening to the discussion).

To begin with, we notice that *well* in broadcast discussion was not as frequent as in interviews and less frequent than in classroom lessons or in business transactions (Table 2.15). About a quarter of the examples were not pragmatic markers. *Well* was typically turn-initial (82.3%), which is a higher figure than for face-to-face (62%) or telephone conversation (42.5%). Differences in position may be related to function but also to who the speaker is and the text type. Fuller (2003: 42), for example, found a high frequency of *well* in interviews which she explained by the use of *well* as a mitigator of a proposition stated by the speaker him- or herself rather than as a coherence marker.[21]

Table 2.15 *Well* in different positions in broadcast discussion

Position	Number	Per cent
Initial	107	82.3%
Initial (after a preceding *yes, yeah, uh(m), right, oh, OK* or a combination of these	4	3.1%
Medial	19	14.6%
Total	130	100%

Well was most frequent in declaratives (96.3%). There were only a few examples in interrogatives or in imperatives (Table 2.16).

Table 2.16 *Well* in different linguistic contexts in broadcast discussion (only clause-initial examples have been counted)

Context	Number	Per cent
Declarative	105	96.3%
Interrogative	3	2.8%
Imperatives	1	0.9%
Total	109	100%

Well was not normally used with pauses (3 examples with a following short or long pause) and one example with a preceding pause.

Table 2.17 shows the distribution of the functions of *well* in broadcast discussion. The functions of *well* are motivated by the text type as suggested by its frequencies in different functions. Below I will discuss the functions of *well* focusing on the transitional function, disagreement and hedging.

Table 2.17 The functions of *well* in broadcast discussion

Function	Number
Coherence	
Transition to a new turn	–
Transition according to an agenda*	65
Direct speech	5
Word-search	7
Self-repair	6
Involvement	
Agree	–
Disagree	38
Insufficient answers	–
Politeness	9
Total	130

* No distinction has been made between transition to a new turn and transition according to an agenda

The functions of *well* in broadcast discussion can be explained by the social activity and the speaker roles. *Well* functions as a contextualisation cue marking a shift to a 'special' function or a transition according to an interpretative frame. As shown in Table 2.17, transitions according to an agenda or a frame are typical of *well* in broadcast discussion. The interpretation of *well* is based on the speakers' background knowledge about what goes on in the broadcast discussion, for example, that new speakers are invited to come in after a certain time in the discussion (an interpretative frame). *Well* as a contextualisation cue indexes functions associated with the roles as moderator or participant in the debate. It was, for example, typically used by the moderator to invite contributions from the discussant (inviting a new speaker) or by the discussant to respond to the moderator and introduce a new topic or aspect of the topic (see below). This explains the differences to a private dialogue where the uses of *well* are not predetermined by the text type. Without *well* and additional markers there might be uncertainty about where a new speaker is supposed to come in. Sub-senses such as disagreeing with a previous speaker do not depend on a particular agenda, although they can be expected to be more frequent in discussion (see below). Moreover, some meanings such as word-search, self-repair and transition to direct speech are found across speech situations and speakers. The low number of examples of *well* with pauses (word-search) and for self-repair reflects the fact that the discussants can be expected to have planned what to say.

To begin with, we notice that *well* was frequent in the coherence function (65% of the examples). One reason is that broadcast discussion is characterised by the explicit signalling of different stages in the activity. *Well* is used together with more elaborate phrases (cf. Stubbs 1983 'prefaces') which 'claim their lack of connectedness to the immediately preceding talk as recognized and therefore accountable' (Stubbs 1983: 184). In particular, prefaces may be an overt sign of the flexibility and 'stretchability' of *well*. Stubbs (1983) provides data from committee meetings and refers to S. Harris (1980) who argues 'that overt references to the discourse and to the speech acts performed are common in courts of law'. The preface is optional (cf. Stubbs 1983: 183). However, the use of extended prefaces is a typical feature of broadcast discussion (and other types of public dialogue) where clarity and explicitness are important. We can make a comparison with conversation where speakers generally prefer shortness in accordance with the Gricean maxim 'be brief (avoid unnecessary prolixity)' (Grice 1975). Principles may be in conflict with each other: in discussion (which is planned to some extent) and is directed to a wide audience the clarity maxim may be more important than to be brief.

Prefaces such as *well let me address that directly, well I tend to agree with you, well do you want me to tell you the reason* signal the transition to a new stage in the discourse (a new topic or argument). However, the function of *well* in broadcast discussion may have less to do with coherence than with signalling a certain stance. *Well* together with a preface can, for example, invest the utterance with authority or knowledgeability:[22]

(42) B: <u>Well let me address that directly</u>
      It seems to me that for instance certainly within the Jewish tradition it's very difficult to identify a concept of the secular in the sense of that which is outside the realm of religion
      On the contrary there there is the realm of the everyday as opposed to the holy
      (S1B-028 0039 – 0041 BROADCAST DISCUSSION)

Both the moderator and the discussants use prefaces but different ones and for different purposes. *Well* in broadcast discussion can be distinguished depending on who uses it. *Well* was used both by the moderator (26 examples) and by the discussants (104 examples) for specific purposes. In broadcast discussion the moderator uses *well* to introduce the issue to be discussed, invite a new speaker to take the floor, to achieve a shift of speakers or topics, to keep the discussion going by asking questions for explanations or clarification, to summarise the discussion so far, or going back in the discourse to resume a topic. See Table 2.18.

Table 2.18 *Well* in different discourse functions in broadcast discussion

Moderator	Discussant
– introducing a controversial issue	– taking the floor for taking a stance, providing an opinion on an issue after an invitation
– inviting a new speaker to take the floor	– making clarifications, explanations
– achieving a shift of speakers or topics	
– asking clarification questions	
– summarising the discussion	
– resuming a topic	

In the following example, the moderator uses *well* in the first move to bring a new speaker into the discussion. The social worker has witnessed cases of sexual child abuse. The issue to be debated is whether children should be removed from their parents:

(44)   A: <u>Well ou our next witness is</u> Judith Dawson
       who's a principal senior social worker in Nottinghamshire
       (S1B-030 0001 BROADCAST DISCUSSION)

The moderator selects a speaker by using *well* followed by the name of the nominated speaker:

(45)   A: <u>Well Terence Hawkes</u> as a professor a university
       professor you must disagree totally with John Major who says common sense is
       the crucial thing not these wretched degrees
       D: Well the trouble with common sense is that it it's it's not common and it's
       often not very sensible either
       (S1B-029 142–143 BROADCAST DISCUSSION)

Well serves as a cue to the hearer to interpret what is said in the context of the broadcast discussion shifting the function to that of nominating a new speaker. *Well* here signals both that the speaker is the moderator and that the transition is to a new stage in the broadcast discussion.

Well precedes phrases for topic shift such as (*turning to you . . ., let's go on to, well let's talk about, well let's move to*):

(46)   A: <u>Well turning to you Tod Handley</u>
       Uhm what first made you interested in music of that particular period
       B: Well in fact I was reading a book
       uh called Musical Trends in the Twentieth Century
       by Norman Demuth
       (S1B-032 011–013 BROADCAST DISCUSSION)

If the speaker is the discussant *well* is used differently. The discussants make clarifications, present, develop or defend a position. *Well* was used by the participant nominated as speaker to signal that an explanation, an argument, or a defence for a certain position is forthcoming related to the issue to be discussed (which is sometimes also introduced by the chairman).

The conversational initiative stays with the speaker until (usually) the chairman comes in to invite a new speaker. In the following example, Melvyn Bragg who is the President of the National Campaign for the Arts (Speaker B) has been invited to discuss whether there should be more governmental funding of the arts. *Well* marks the opening to his contribution to the discussion. The answer in response the moderator's question is to talk about the poor finances of the arts.

(47)   A: Melvyn Bragg you're President of the National Campaign for the Arts the lead
        signatory in the letter part of which I quoted a few moments ago
        What do you think's gone wrong <,>
        B: <u>Well</u> before we start to talk about finances which'll occupy a lot of this pro-
        gramme and blame which'll occupy a lot of this programme the reason why I'm
        we're here and people are watching is because most people think that the arts
        add something to their lives that nothing else will give them
        (S1B-022 0012–0014 BROADCAST DISCUSSION)

The speaker could have started his contribution without *well*. However, in that case the possibility of signalling both authority and the intention to take the floor for an extensive argument would have been lost. *Well* introduces a 'narrative answer' especially when the question is a *wh*-question (Hale 1999: 59). The examples typically occur at the beginning of the discussion and coincide with the introduction of a new speaker.

Example (48) is also from a discussion. Monica is asked to provide her opinion on the existence of 'spirit guides' dictating a novel. The broadcast discussion is similar to a monologue in that the invited speaker is allowed to speak uninterrupted.

(48)   A: Monica you're a writer
        What do you make of all this
        Are <unclear>from the other side
        B: <u>Well I believe</u> that anything is possible because we have no proof that it isn't
        (S1B-026 231–234 BROADCAST DISCUSSION)

Monica has been invited as an established writer. By using *well* she conveys assertiveness and authority.

Other functions such as disagreeing with a previous speaker do not depend on a particular interpretative frame, although *well* with a disagreeing function is more frequent in discussion than in face-to-face conversation and is typically used by the discussants. This is to be expected since the participants are invited because they hold divergent viewpoints and are supposed to provide arguments for or against a certain point. In (49) *well* is used to introduce an objection or a counter-argument:

(49)   F: In the in
        D: It's not what I said actually
        F: <u>Well</u> something like that You said after after the war's declared
        we should uh that information should be controlled
        (S1B-031 131–134 BROADCAST DISCUSSION)

The topic discussed in (50) is the Tory leadership contest as fought in newspapers and on TV and, in particular, whether there was 'any pleasure in it'. Disagreement can be softened and, if it is built on a misunderstanding, corrected. In (50) *well* is associated with error correction. Speaker F, Michael Dobbs, has worked as an assistant to Margaret Thatcher:

(50) A: Uh you don't take any pleasure in this do you Michael
     F: <u>Well</u> not pleasure because I actually happen to think unlike most
     people here that there is a serious side to politics
     (S1B-024 0045–0046 BROADCAST DISCUSSION)

Well (not pleasure) is used to correct the previous speaker.

In (51) the speaker avoids disagreement by answering the question indirectly. *Well* introducing a correction or counter-argument to the preceding discourse is also to be expected in a broadcast discussion:

(51) A: If you don't accept that ACPO is accountable
     to nobody who is it accountable to
     C: <u>Well</u> it isn't accountable on the basis that
     it merely is a group of Chief Constables
     who sit down together to consider the new
     issues and and devise if you like systems
     of policing what is best in terms of
     a common policy
     (S1B-033 078–079 BROADCAST DISCUSSION)

Combinations such as *well . . . but (well . . . and yet, well . . . on the other hand)* suggest that the discussion is characterised by reasoning and deliberation rather than by open conflict or disagreement.

(52) A: Mm
     B: Yeah
     A: <u>Well</u> I suppose there is
     A: <u>But</u> wasn't it true at that time that
     a great many British composers composed in a
     continental vein I mean following Brahms or <,>
     whatever
     B: Yeah
     C: Well I think those influences were were fairly
     obvious
     (S1B-032–040 BROADCAST DISCUSSION)

In (53) *well* is used strategically to first claim acceptance of the preceding utterance and then to claim the opposite.

(53) E: <u>Well I I agree precisely with what Paddy
     Ashdown said just now</u>

It would be devoutly to be wished that
his military might was greatly damaged
But uh I think the authority that the
United Nations was given is that he should
withdraw from Kuwait or be made to withdraw
from Kuwait
and that's what we have to do
(S1B-027 072–075 BROADCAST DISCUSSION)

The following examples with *well* have been analysed as hedges since they reflect the speaker's wish to modify the force of the assertion. The participants use *well certainly*, *well actually*, *well I am sure*, *well I think*, *well I believe that*, *well I mean*, *well there's no doubt at all that*, *well of course* to take up a position and to identify themselves as authorities on a certain topic. *Well* is associated with certainty and knowledgeability rather than with impoliteness.

In (54) the topic is the role of religion in contemporary society. B and C are the participants in the debate.

(54)   B: I tried to speak about religion in general in contemporary society rather than
       from within one particular religious tradition [. . .] maybe some of the subjects I
       discussed really are of significant importance
       C: Well there can certainly be no doubt that one has general importance that uh
       runs through all of the faiths and that is this general idea that uh secularisation
       means something <,>
       (S1B-028 009-0011 BROADCAST DISCUSSION)

Speaker C could have said 'one has general importance that runs through all the faiths'. By using *well* and *certainly there can be no doubt* the speaker qualifies the force of the assertion that secularisation means something to all religious faiths. Without *well* the speaker's argument would have sounded rude.

In a broadcast discussion the function of *well* is to take up an authoritative stance without offending the hearer. In (55) the topic for discussion is whether the farmer or a conservation society is best qualified to manage the preservation of footpaths. The moderator A leaves the floor to Sir Simon Growley who argues in his capacity as a landowner in favour of leaving the care to the farmers:

(55)   A: But who do you think is best qualified to manage that conservation
       Is it the pressure group like the Open
       Spaces Society or is it the farmer
       B: Well I think it's unquestionably the farmer because uh <,> the landscape has
       got to be farmed otherwise it will degenerate into something
       which people <,> don't recognise
       (S1B-037 097 BROADCAST DISCUSSION)

In the combination *well but* the function of *well* is to change disagreement into something more harmless by softening or qualifying what is said. The medium has appeared as a 'spirit guide' dictating a story to D. Speaker A is now arguing that the story dictated would not have been as good as the genuine thing although the 'Maupassant story' was quite good.

(56)   D: And so it's bound to come out in the terms she would use
       A: <u>Well</u> <u>but</u> it's very uneven because I mean the Maupassant story is actually quite Maupassant and quite good
       (S1B-026 121–124 BROADCAST DISCUSSION)

Well suggests that the speaker has considered alternative views without actively opposing other views. This makes *well* different from the simple *but* which is used to make a contrast between two conflicting positions explicit. According to Carlson (1984: 44):

> [*well*] can be construed as giving due consideration to the opposing view without implying acceptance of the view itself. More importantly, *well* does not make the contrast between the two viewpoints explicit in the way *but* does; *well* is ater [sic] all used in many other ways too, introducing harmless remarks as well as challenging moves. It lets the listener work out the conclict [sic] between his position and the new contribution.

A broadcast discussion is a fairly routinised activity following an agenda and associated with special speaker roles. *Well* therefore functions as a contextualisation cue marking shifts to a special function or interpretative frame. Moreover, *well* was frequently found with prefaces identifying the speaker 'as the incumbent of a social role' (Stubbs 1983: 160). For example, the moderator uses *well* to control the discussion. The contributors on the other hand use *well* to signal that they are responding to the moderator and are about to defend a particular position. *Well* is also used for hedging (mitigating illocutionary force), to establish a social or professional role and to create an image of the speaker as authoritative and knowledgeable. As may be expected a prototypical or salient function of *well* in discussion is to soften disagreement. *Well* has the effect of changing disagreement into 'reasoning with deliberation'. In other words, rudeness is not expected or appropriate in broadcast discussion.

Well was more frequent in initial position in the discussions, which can be related to its turn–introductory functions (introducing a turn, topic, speaker, etc.). It was more frequent in answers than in conversation. *Well*, however, introduces a narrative answer and has the function to signal professional status and expertise.

2.12.2 *Well* in cross-examination

Well was infrequent in cross-examination in the ICE-GB Corpus, chiefly because of the small sample of cross-examinations in the corpus. *Well* was initial in 44 examples and medial only in 8 examples. *Well* typically occurred without pauses (1 example with a preceding short pause, 3 examples with *uh(m)*, 1 example with *yeah*).

A cross-examination is built up mainly of questions and answers. The questions and answers are sequentially ordered and controlled by the prosecutor or the defence counsel whose goal it is to show that the defendant's (or plaintiff's) claim is invalid. The distribution of *well* depending on whether the context is a statement, question, answer or request is shown in Table 2.19:

Table 2.19 *Well* in different speech act contexts

Context	Number	Per cent
Statement	9	17.3%
Question	22	42.3%
Answer	18	34.6%
Request	3	5.8%
Total	52	100%

All the speakers used *well* but with different frequencies and with different functions. The prosecutor/defence counsel used *well* 28 times and the witness who was cross-examined used it 22 times. The questions and answers were also used differently and with different frequencies by the participants in the examination. The defendant (witness) for example asks no questions. In the ICE-GB all the questions introduced by *well* were asked by the examiner.[23]

Some functions are shared with face-to-face conversation (and other text types), such as self-repair ('shifting gear' in order to self-correct or bring in some information parenthetically), and introducing direct speech. Other functions were specific to the text type and are associated with an interpretative frame. As shown in Table 2.20, *well* is primarily a coherence device.

Table 2.20 The functions of *well* in cross-examinations

Function	Number
Coherence	
Transitional according to an agenda	44
Direct speech	2
Word-search	
Self-repair	4
Involvement	
Agreeing	1
Disagreeing	1
Insufficient answer	–
Politeness	–
Total	52

Special uses can be explained by the function of *well* as a contextualisation device. *Well* signals a shift to a question (by the prosecutor) or the response to the question (by the defendant). The frequency of *well* in questions is noteworthy. We can make a comparison with face-to-face conversation where *well* is used differently. By using *well* in questions the speaker can appear friendly. However, in the courtroom the opposite may be the case. *Well* can be a sign of power and aggressiveness depending on who uses it. Hale (1999), for example, has drawn attention to the fact that *well* in questions (and requests) can be aggressive – at least in the examples she studied from court examinations. The following example is from a cross-examination (a question-answer session) in the ICE-GB – a context where *well* introduces the examiner's questions.

According to the witness, actions had been taken to arrange a mortgage by a certain date. That leads to the examiner's questions whether it was understood that the witness examined should have the money by then.

> (57) A: And you didn't say *that's not what we agreed*
> B: No As far as I was aware the completion date would be the third of February and we'd taken all action necessary to arrange the mortgage offer before that date
> A: <u>Well</u> did you understand from Mr Sainsbury that if you didn't have money by the third of February it would cause problems
> (S1B-061 157–160 CROSS EXAMINATION)

In 8 examples a tag-question construction was used. In (58) the prosecutor uses a tag question coercing the defendant to confirm the description he presents of the facts:

> (58) A: <u>Well</u> he's certainly not called you to
> buy uh to sell his business lock stock
> and barrel <u>has he</u>
> (S1B-064 159 CROSS EXAMINATION)

Well reflects a change to a new stage in the cross-examination and is also used to underline who is in control (in power). The function of *well* (to introduce a challenging question) can only be understood against the background of our knowledge of what goes on in a cross-examination and the role of the speaker as prosecutor or defendant.

Depending on the situation different inferences can be made about what *well* means. In ordinary conversation the tone is not aggressive. It can be argued that in conversation where *well* was infrequent in questions it tends to be mitigating:

> (59) B: Well they obviously don't approve of it and they're all <,> in the same boat really
> A: <u>Well</u> when you're saying thefts is it large quantities or just the occasional
> B: It's just the occasional
> (S1A-059 132–134 FACE)

The witness, on the other hand, used *well* when denying something (= 'yes but') or to express a diverging opinion (Hale 1999: 60):

> (60) B: It wasn't put like that <,,>
> A: Wasn't put like that <,>
> So uh <,> if it had been put
> like that you might have taken a different
> attitude
> is that what you're saying
> B: <u>Well no</u>
> My attitude was <,> in that particular instance

the fact that uh th the media w
uhm brickwork had been taken down in the
corner of the blue and brown wall <,>
(S1B-069 156–161 CROSS EXAMINATION)

Well in the witness's answers to questions is associated with 'fighting back' or correcting a misunderstanding rather than with agreement or confirmation. In both cases the defendant denies the presuppositions on which the questions are based.

To summarise, we have seen that there are general differences in the frequency of *well* in cross-examination compared with other text types (in particular with informal conversation). *Well* has many situational interpretations. The contextual factors interacting with *well* are different in the courtroom from conversation. They refer, for example, to speaker roles (as prosecutor and defendant), the organisation of the cross-examination into questions and answers, the social goal associated with the activity (winners and losers). The functions of *well* in questions follow from our knowledge of the goal of a cross-examination, how it is built up of questions and answers and who says what. *Well* in questions is used for 'fighting'; it is associated with control and a particular speaker role.

The discourse type (social situation or activity type) does not only constrain the functions of *well* but it conveys information about where *well* is used (and by whom) thus helping the hearer to interpret what is said. *Well* is used as a contextualisation cue signalling the transition to a new function, new speaker, new activity. It serves as a resource for the speaker (for example the prosecutor in the courtroom) to build up a professional identity. The prosecutor selects *well* when asking questions because it allows him or her to express a number of social or indexical meanings.

2.14 *Well* in spontaneous commentaries

The spontaneous commentaries in the ICE-GB corpus are mostly taken from radio broadcast commentaries on sports events (soccer, rugby, cricket, bicycle or sidecar racing). Two of the texts are rather commentaries on public events. In all there were 73 examples of the pragmatic marker *well* in commentaries. In the examples chosen for illustration there is a commentator reporting 'spontaneously' what goes on in the game.

We have few analyses of pragmatic markers in commentaries (Greasley's 1994 analysis of commentaries on a snooker game is an exception). There are some similarities with the categories postulated by Müller (2005) to describe how *well* was used by informants (German learners and American students) in the retelling of a silent Chaplin movie. However, some functions are particular to the sports commentary.

The functions of *well* can be derived from expectations of, or background knowledge about, the sports commentary. In the (sports) commentary there is a commentator who is an expert on the game monitoring the progress of the event. The commentator reports what takes place to a broadcast audience (players miss the ball, new players enter the field, etc.). He also provides evaluations (*that's a good tackle*), describes reactions to something unexpected or remarkable, explains or analyses the game and provides general background knowledge on the players and the game (*X has won simply everything this year, we've now accepted 56 of the 83 laps, X didn't make it last year in the World Cup*). *Well* is also an important cue drawing attention to the shift from one activity to another.

To begin with, we can make some observations about the formal properties of *well* in spontaneous commentaries. It was used with unfilled pauses in 10 examples and with *uh* in 9 examples. *Well* collocated with *and* in 3 examples and occurred in the pattern *and uh well* in 4 examples.

The commentary is not organised into topics and does not follow a pre-fixed agenda but is a moment-to-moment commentary on what happens in the game. *Well* typically accompanies the commentary punctuating it in places where the commentator chooses to come in. However, the commentator is also supposed to analyse and evaluate what goes on. The functions I have distinguished in Table 2.21 can therefore also be derived from our background knowledge about sports commentaries (a sports commentary frame). They will be further described below.

Table 2.21 The functions of *well* in spontaneous commentaries

Function	Number
Coherence	
Ongoing commentary	32
Self-repair	5
Introducing a new player	4
Involvement	
Asides	14
Opinion or evaluation	7
Analysis	10
Total	72

When *well* signals that the commentator is attending to the game moment by moment it can be inserted in many places in the utterance (32 examples):

(61) A: Well there was certainly an infringement
     Samways <,> <u>well strokes it back to Mabbutt</u>
     And the tackle was well timed by David Hillier
     (S2A-015 012–015 SPONTANEOUS COMMENTARY)

The punctuating function of *well* is characteristic of commentaries. It can be compared with word-search in conversation but represents a special use in commentaries where it is associated with what the speaker can observe:

(62) A: Dixon gets that cross in
     headed away <u>well there by Kalatsakas and uh</u>
     <u>well finally hammered away</u> deep into the Arsenal
     half but uh straight through to David Seaman
     and Seaman will just play it short for
     Bould Bould had an excellent season last year
     (S2A-018 254–257 SPONTANEOUS COMMENTARY)

And well is used to summarise a description of what happens and could also have been regarded as a special category:

(63) A: They played last Friday at uh Plymouth which
       was a very physical game by all accounts
       And all these players out here playing for
       first team places
       And well possible defensive slip-up there
       Ball let the ball go and uh well
       Seaman had to be extremely quick and agile
       there to dive at the feet of the Greek forward
       (S2A-018 019–022 SPONTANEOUS COMMENTARY)

The pronunciation of *well* could further be used to characterise the speaker. *Well* in (63) was pronounced with a slight drawl indicating that the commentator does not speak light-heartedly. In the same example (*uh*) *well* was pronounced with a falling tone.

The commentator can express a reaction to his own talk. Repairs occur when the commentator modifies or replaces his account with something else:

(64) A: The flag stays down
       No it doesn't
       Well in fact the flag stayed down because
       the linesman dropped his flag in trying to
       raise it
       (S2A-015–017 SPONTANEOUS COMMENTARY)

In (65) an earlier formulation is replaced by a more precise one:

(65) A: Surely offside <,>
       long way offside
       Well <,> forty metres offside
       (S2A-002 168–172 SPONTANEOUS COMMENTARY)

In the following example *uh well* signals a reanalysis of the situation:

(66) A: And there's plenty of green shirts there
       And uh Vasiche was ready for a shot
       which uh Well Arsenal blocked the danger
       Come away on that far side with Rocastle
       Slips it up to halfway
       (S2A-018 050–055 SPONTANEOUS COMMENTARY)

There were also examples where the speaker used *well* before an answer to a self-posed question (cf. Müller 2004: 1168):

(67) A: Edge of the penalty area
       Oh and was that a penalty
       Well there was certainly an infringement

No
The referee allows play to go on
(S2A-014 248–252 SPONTANEOUS COMMENTARY)

In (68) the commentator introduces the 'world record holder on the scene' (*well here is*):

(68) A: <u>Well here is</u> the world record holder Willy
Banks who in fact is some way down
from his uh leading form now fifteen metres
fifty-eight in the first round
and he holds the world record at seventeen
metres ninety-seven
(S2A-007 072–073 SPONTANEOUS COMMENTARY)

The commentator uses *well* to signal that Andy Gregory has entered the field (having an altercation with another player):

(69) <u>Well</u> <,,> <u>Well</u> little uh Andy Gregory <u>there</u>
Having an altercation with Glen Lazarus
(S2A-004 142–144 SPONTANEOUS COMMENTARY)

An aside conveys some general information or background knowledge (e.g. how often the two teams have met in the past). It has been considered a special use of *well* in commentaries. An equally important function of *well* is to convey the speaker's expertise in a particular area:

(70) A: And it's gone behind away to our right for a goal kick to the Soviet Union
<u>Well</u> this is the eleventh meeting between the
two countries
(S2A-001 164–166 SPONTANEOUS COMMENTARY)

According to Greasley (1994: 484), *well* is addressed to 'a situation that warranted analysis and assessment'. Greasley analysed commentaries on snooker. Here are some examples of the commentator's analysis of a soccer game:

(71) A: Not quite clear
And in comes Geoff Thomas
<u>Well he hammered it</u>
He had to hit it early because uh
Kuznecov it was was coming in with a with a quick tackle <,>
(S2A-001 025–028 SPONTANEOUS COMMENTARY)

(72) A: <u>Well they're a goal down at the
moment</u> <,>
England nil
Soviet Union one
(S2A-001 072–073 SPONTANEOUS COMMENTARY)

In 7 examples *well* introduced an evaluation. The commentator is supposed not only to report what is happening but to evaluate it. We can compare face-to-face conversations where speakers agree or disagree with a preceding statement rather than evaluate it.

(73) A: Right-footed
      Sweeps it long
      <u>Well that was a lovely ball by Mark Wright</u>
      (S2A-001 060-062 SPONTANEOUS COMMENTARY)

In (74) the commentator could have reported the same sequence of events without *well* but this would have sounded less involved and the report would have been less likely to catch the audience's interest:

(74) A: Well Steven knew that unless he got the
      cue ball behind the green he was going
      to leave <,> Mike a chance of the
      cut <,,>
      <u>Well that is cruel</u> <,,> and uh one
      has to feel very sorry for Mike Hallet <,,>
      (S2A-008 069–070 SPONTANEOUS COMMENTARY)

Evaluations can be positive or negative:

(75) A: <u>Well that really is the worst possible start</u>
      as far as Rangers are concerned because their
      team already shows uh a fair amount of
      deficiencies at the back there without Andy Tilson
      and Darren Peacock who are both cup-tied since
      their early season moves from Grimsby and Hereford
      respectively
      (S2A-003 067 SPONTANEOUS COMMENTARY)

To sum up, we can explain many new uses of *well* on the basis of the commentator's role in the discourse and the presence of an audience who cannot see what is happening in the game. The commentator views what is going on in a game and is supposed to explain and analyse the players' actions and deliberations for an audience who can only follow the game on the radio. *Well* is used by commentators in 'specialised functions' which could be explained by the constraints imposed by the commentary, in particular, by the speed with which it has to be delivered and the demands of fluency. *Well* is, for instance, needed by the commentator to take stock of the situation and draw attention to what is happening in the game. *Well* as a pause marker was pronounced with a full vowel and could be phonologically varied.

In the broadcast commentary, *well* is used typically to comment on shifts or changes in the game. *Well* is used, for example, to highlight a new event, draw attention to a new player on the field, an unexpected situation or development in the game (X lets go of the ball, X is ready for a shot, etc.). *Well* was also used by the commentator to take stock of the situation before analysing or explaining what takes place.

The analysis of *well* in commentaries shows additional reasons and possibilities for using *well* depending on the activity type, speaker role, the purpose of the activity. *Well* with a coherence function is, for instance, used to comment on new episodes in the game. In comparison with face-to-face conversation *well* was often used for evaluation. We can generalise and say that the usefulness of certain functions is motivated by the situation. The specific functions of *well* in the commentary are not new sub-senses but contextual adaptations or extensions.

2.14 Conclusion

The best way to deal with recalcitrant markers such as *well*, which varies its function depending on the situation, is to investigate the pragmatic marker in as many different contexts as possible. The inclusion of a number of new contexts shows 'that it is always possible for a speaker of a language to use an item in a somewhat innovative way in some-what similar functions or context, rendering the meaning of each and every item not a ready-made unit but a constantly developing and renewed potential' (Keevallik 2003: 342).

Well provides a number of 'opportunities for use' (Linell 2009: 347). At least in infor-mal conversation the meanings of *well* are more or less conventionalised senses. When we consider other text types and situations the same senses can be stretched or modified, a particular function can be missing or can be overridden by another function. The use of a moderator controlling turn-taking and speaking time as in broadcast discussion may lead to more fine-grained functions of *well*, for example, to introduce a new contribution to the discussion (a new speaker, etc.). *Well* is associated both with specialised functions and with transitions according to an agenda (specifying the overall organisation of the activity type).

The theory of meaning potentials provides a general description of how meanings are organised around several sub-senses and how the meanings are related on the basis of different types of polysemy. A number of sub-senses (core functions) have been distin-guished and classified on the basis of their association with general contextual parameters such as coherence, involvement and politeness. New sub-senses can develop when *well* is used in different contexts. The new functions can be 'weak' only (that is, less convention-alised. This becomes apparent if *well* collocates with another element in a particular func-tion. In the combination *well I mean* I have, for instance, categorised *well* as an example of self-repair. The context also includes stance. *Well* can convey affective stance (feelings of reluctance, or 'friendliness') as well as epistemic stance (authority, knowledge, challenge). In an informal conversation pragmatic markers such as *well* are used as 'specific instru-ments for partners' co-operation' (Weydt 2006) but the opposite might be the case in a discussion where speakers disagree. *Well* is used to establish authority and power and to take up positions such as challenging an idea or another speaker.

However, speakers do not only select a function of *well*. They also exploit its formal variability. *Well* is short, it can be placed initially or in medial position depending on its function. Both pronunciation and pausing are clues to the function of *well*. Factors like speed and a 'drawling' pronunciation or a certain intonation are also part of the picture presented to the hearer. However, prosodic factors are not used systematically or conven-tionally to convey a certain meaning of *well*. On the other hand, they can be exploited for affective meanings of *well* such as reluctance or disappointment.

This study should only be seen as a beginning. We need many more fine-grained studies of *well* in different social situations. A number of contextual factors have been seen to interact with the choice of *well*, for example the medium (telephone conversation), the turn-taking organisation (broadcast discussion), the agenda (cross-examination), social roles and professional identities (broadcast discussion, cross-examination), the presence of an audience (broadcast discussion, spontaneous commentary), the overall organisation of the discourse (broadcast discussion, courtroom examination, spontaneous commentary). We can expect many more factors to play a role in how *well* is used.

Notes

1. Some important milestones in the study of *well* are R. Lakoff (1973), Halliday and Hasan (1976), Wierzbicka (1976), Svartvik (1980), Schiffrin (1987), Bolinger (1989), Watts (1989), Jucker (1993), Carlson (1984), Schourup (2001). Compare also the discussion of *well* in works dealing with contexts other than conversation. *Well* has also been studied contrastively on the basis of parallel corpora in different languages (Aijmer and Simon-Vandenbergen 2003, Johansson 2006) and in learner language (Aijmer 2011).
2. In a diachronic perspective, however, it is quite possible that *well* as a pragmatic marker is associated with the propositional *well*. See Defour (2009).
3. Defour (2009: 167), on the other hand, associates the meaning 'consideration' with 'well well' which is tied 'to the propositional use of *well*, which inherently entails a subjective judgement and as such establishes a norm that requires the speaker to engage in a process of active consideration'.
4. Müller compared German EFL learners' use of *well* with American native speakers of English.
5. Data from the Diachronic Corpus of Present-Day Spoken English (DCPSE) contains spoken material from the London-Lund Corpus and the British Component of the ICE-Corpus. It consists of c. 400,000 words from each of the two corpora.
6. The COLT Corpus focuses on the speech of teenagers. It was collected in 1993 and has the same size as the LLC (500,000 words). See Stenström, Andersen and Hasund (2002).
7. The participants were mainly Hong Kong Chinese speakers of English.
8. Only examples of the pragmatic marker have been counted.
9. Cf. also Bazzanella (2006) for a functional model for pragmatic markers distinguishing between a cognitive, interactional and metatextual function of pragmatic markers. Bazzanella further subdivides the macro-functions into different micro-functions based on her Italian data (2006: 456).
10. Fischer (2000: 100) arrives at eight different functional categories (sub-senses or core aspects) of *well*: take-up, back-channel, framer, repair marker, answer, action, check and modal. However, the principles for distinguishing these functions (and not others) are unclear.
11. In Brinton's framework (1996) the involvement and politeness function would be subsumed under the interpersonal function.
12. *Well* in incomplete utterances such as *well I* (followed by the complete *well I think*)

has been regarded as a separate category by Svartvik (1980). I have classified both examples of *well* as 'self-repair'.

13. According to Bolinger (1989: 321), this category 'corresponds to Schiffrin's "aliveness to the need to accomplish coherence" (ibid. 662) and Svartvik's "something in common with what went before." The speaker gives the nod to the state of affairs then current, accepting it as background, and goes on to add something.'

14. However, 'we can also attribute other functions to *well* in utterances where there is also explicit delay' (Innes 2010: 106).

15. Carlson's (1984: 49) 'subdued acceptance'.

16. Cf. Bolinger (1989: 319) who notes that combinations such as *well therefore, well yet* and *well so* are unacceptable because 'the other modifier is oriented away from what is prior or extant'.

17. Compare also Fuller (2003: 41) who found that *well* occurred turn-initially or after a preceding discourse marker in 69% of the examples.

18. Initial position includes examples of *well* (or *well* with a preceding *uh(m)* with no clause attached).

19. 4 examples occurred after other question types mainly confirmation questions introduced by *so* with or without a tag question.

20. Unclear examples have not been counted.

21. Position is typically text-specific. *Well* is for instance used turn medially more often in interviews than in conversation according to Fuller (2003).

22. Stubbs (1983), on the other hand, associates *well* in prefaces with mitigation. His examples are, however, from committee meetings.

23. In 6 examples the question had the form of an assertion.

3

In Fact and *Actually* – A Class of Adversative Pragmatic Markers

3.1 Introduction

In fact and *actually* are closely related. There are many similarities between them. They have the same etymological meaning and they share many functions. They have mainly been discussed diachronically. Traugott and Dasher (2002) traced the development of *actually, in fact* (and *indeed*) from VP adverbials to sentential adverbials and further to pragmatic markers both in a macro-perspective and on the micro-level and found subtle differences in their history which show up as synchronic differences (cf. also Powell 1992). The present study is synchronic only and focuses on the variability and flexibility of *in fact* (and *actually*) in different text types and social situations and the formal, functional and contextual features constraining their usage. The hypothesis which will be explored is that it is the social situation rather than shared literal meaning which determines how the pragmatic markers are used. Such a study can also throw light on what the factors are constraining their usage.

In fact and *actually* have been referred to as modal adverbs (cf. Quirk et al. 1985 'disjuncts'), as both modal adverbs and discourse markers by Schwenter and Traugott (2000), and as pragmatic markers (discourse markers) by Fraser (1996). It is, however, difficult to distinguish between the modal adverb and the pragmatic marker formally and functionally and it is not useful for the aims of this study to make such a distinction. I have therefore opted to refer to them as pragmatic markers.

The chapter is organised as follows. Section 3.2 deals with previous work. Section 3.3 shows the distribution of *in fact* and *actually* over different corpora and in different text types. Section 3.4 is an introduction to *in fact* and deals with its formal features (formal and prosodic features, collocation). Section 3.5 discusses the functions of *in fact* mainly in conversation. Sections 3.6–3.8 deal with *in fact* in a selection of other text types and situations. Section 3.9 summarises the discussion of *in fact*. Section 3.10 introduces *actually* and deals with its formal features. 3.11 discusses its functional properties mainly in conversation summarised in Section 3.12. Sections 3.13–3.15 deal with *actually* in some other text types where it is frequent. Section 3.16 summarises the analysis of *actually*. Section 3.17 contrasts the formal and contextual features constraining the usage of *in fact* and *actually*.

3.2 Previous work

In fact and *actually* have often been discussed together and show both similarities and differences. Oh (2000: 243) for example claims that *actually* and *in fact* develop a number of uses from a core meaning ('unexpectedness') 'in real discourse contexts'. The study uses the Switchboard corpus (American English telephone conversations) and the Brown Corpus (written American English). Oh demonstrated that *actually* was more frequent than *in fact* in spoken American English and that the markers preferred different positional patterns. When she compared the functions of *in fact* and *actually* she found that there was a tendency for *in fact* to be upgrading or strengthening while *actually* was more typically used to deny an expectation. Oh's study is also interesting because it points to a stylistic difference in the use of *actually* and *in fact* based on their occurrence in informative versus imaginative prose in the Brown Corpus. Both *actually* and *in fact* were more frequent in informative prose than in imaginative prose. However imaginative prose preferred *actually* to *in fact* which may relate to the fact that it was used more often in fiction which is closer to spoken discourse (Oh 2000: 263).

Mortier and Degand (2009) studied both French *en fait* (in fact) and Dutch *eigenlijk* (actually). They regard the meaning of *eigenlijk* and *en fait* as 'adversative', at the interface between 'opposition' and 'reformulation' which constitute their basic meanings (core meanings) and from which other meanings can be derived. They also point to the 'feeble' (or 'non-absolute') meaning of the markers which allows them to occur in many different contexts. However, their data is primarily written. We can therefore expect differences in the spoken register: 'one can hypothesize that *eigenlijk* as well as *en fait* have a different status in spontaneous conversation, which may well illustrate an ongoing loosening of constraints in informal speech' (Mortier and Degand 2009: 363). Mortier and Degand's analysis is also interesting because they show that a contrastive analysis (French-Dutch) can help us to establish the diversity of meanings of the markers. In the present chapter it will be shown how we can arrive at an even richer description of the markers by considering their uses in different text types (and in spoken rather than written language).

Schwenter and Traugott (2000) focus on the development of *in fact* but their analysis is also interesting for a description of the synchronic uses of *actually*. For example, they draw attention to the fact that *in fact* can be regarded as three-ways polysemous[1]. In the epistemic meaning *in fact* combines aspects of the meanings of *certainly* and *however*. It indexes (strong) epistemic commitment on a scale where weaker commitment is expressed by *probably* and *possibly*. *In fact* can also be a discourse marker 'bracketing segments of discourse' (Schiffrin 1987) doing metatextual work 'allowing speakers to display their rhetorical strategies' (Schwenter and Traugott 2000: 12).

3.3 Distribution of *in fact* and *actually* over text types

The study is based on the British component of the ICE Corpus (the ICE-GB Corpus) which contains both speech and writing, dialogue and monologue and represents a number of different text types and social situations (cf. Chapter 1, 1.3).

Both *in fact* and *actually* were significantly more frequent in speech than in writing. The difference was significant at p<.001.[2] However *actually* was more frequent than *in fact* in both speech and writing (Table 3.1).

Table 3.1 Frequencies of *in fact* and *actually* in speech and writing in the ICE–GB

	In fact		*Actually*		
	Frequency	Per 1,000,000	Frequency	Per 1,000,000	Number of words in the ICE-GB
Speech	330	518	928	1,455	637,682
Writing	78	184	93	220	423,581

In Oh's data (2000: 247), the frequencies of *in fact* in speech and writing were almost the same (0.014% versus 0.015%). *Actually*, on the other hand, was about 3.4 times more frequent in spoken than in written English in her data (to be compared with 4.3 times more frequent in the ICE–GB). The frequencies of *in fact* and *actually* in speech and writing in the ICE–GB can be compared to those in the British National Corpus (100 million words; c. 10 million speech and c. 90 million words of writing). *In fact* was almost twice as frequent in speech as in writing and *actually* more than eight times as frequent in spoken language (Table 3.2).

Table 3.2 Frequencies of *in fact* and *actually* in speech and writing in the British National Corpus (BNC)

	In fact		*Actually*		
	Frequency	Per 1,000,000	Frequency	Per 1,000,000	Number of words in the BNC
Speech	2,994	288	12,773	1,227	10,409,858
Writing	13,327	151	12,640	144	87,903,571
Total	16,321	439	25,413	1,371	98,313,429

The distribution of the markers over different types of texts in speech and writing is shown in Tables 3.3 and 3.4.

Actually was more frequent than *in fact* in direct conversation, telephone calls, classroom lessons, broadcast discussions and interviews, business transactions, unscripted speeches, demonstrations, broadcast news and broadcast talks. *In fact,* on the other hand, was more frequent in parliamentary debates, legal cross-examinations, spontaneous commentaries, legal presentations, and non-broadcast speeches. The frequencies are different for monologue and dialogue.

Table 3.3 *In fact* and *actually* in the spoken part of the ICE-GB

	In fact		Actually		
	Frequency	Per 1,000,000	Frequency	Per 1,000,000	Number of words
Private (dialogue)					
Direct conversation	68	367	392	2,116	185,208
Telephone calls	5	244	46	2,252	20,419
Public (dialogue)					
Classroom lessons	20	473	98	2,321	42,210
Broadcast discussions	29	660	72	1,639	43,920
Broadcast interviews	9	406	37	1,670	22,147
Parliamentary debates	10	474	6	284	21,060
Legal cross-examinations	32	1,510	23	1,085	21,179
Business transactions	10	486	54	2,628	20,546
Unscripted monologue					
Spontaneous commentaries	19	447	12	282	42,466
Unscripted speeches	55	832	103	1,559	66,065
Demonstrations	30	1,329	53	2,348	22,563
Legal presentations	15	690	2	92	21,735
Mixed					
Broadcast news	2	46	9	209	43,061
Scripted monologues					
Broadcast talks	8	22	16	367	43,506
Non-broadcast speeches	14	648	3	138	21,597

Table 3.4 *In fact* and *actually* in monologue and dialogue

	In fact		Actually		
	Frequency	Per 1,000,000	Frequency	Per 1,000,000	Number of words
Dialogue	193	512	728	1,933	376,689
Monologue (scripted and unscripted)	183	840	189	867	217,932
Total	376	1,352	917	2,800	594,621

In fact occurred more often in monologue than in dialogue. The difference is significant at $p < .001$. *Actually* on the other hand was found more frequently in dialogue than in monologue. The difference is significant at $p < .001$.

The distribution of the two markers over text types in the written part of the ICE-GB is shown in Table 3.5.

Table 3.5 The frequency of *in fact* and *actually* in written texts

	In fact		*Actually*		
	Frequency	Per 1,000,000	Frequency	Per 1,000,000	Number of words
Correspondence					
Business letters	11	360	1	32	30,491
Social letters	8	257	19	611	31,085
Non-professional writing					
Student examination scripts	5	235	8	376	21,225
Untimed student essays	4	187	1	46	21,304
Academic writing					
Humanities	5	230	7	322	21,722
Natural sciences	6	280	2	93	21,381
Social sciences	4	189	7	330	21,163
Technology	1	46	1	46	21,320
Creative writing					
Novels/stories	6	140	8	187	42,646
Instructional writing					
Administrative/regulatory	–	–	6	283	21,142
Skills/hobbies	5	235	2	94	21,199
Non-academic writing					
Humanities	2	84	10	423	23,587
Natural sciences	4	191	3	143	20,841
Social sciences	7	332	9	427	21,038
Technology	3	141	4	188	21,179
Persuasive writing					
Press editorials	2	48	2	48	20,719
Reportage					
Press news reports	5	120	3	72	41,539

The frequencies are generally low. We notice, however, a tendency for *in fact* to be more frequent than *actually* in business letters, untimed student essays, natural science (academic and non-academic) writing, skills and hobbies and press news reports. *Actually* was most frequent in social letters (where it was more frequent than *in fact*).

The variability of *actually* and *in fact* is also shown by the fact that they can become more or less frequent over time. Table 3.6 compares the frequencies of *in fact* and *actually* in the Diachronic Corpus of Present-day Spoken English (DCPSE)[3].

Table 3.6 Frequencies of *in fact* and *actually* in the DCPSE (the London-Lund corpus and the ICE-GB corpus). The figures have been normalised to 1,000,000 words.

	In fact		*Actually*		
	Frequency	Per 1,000,000	Frequency	Per 1,000,000	Number of words
ICE-GB	204	473	718	1,665	431,262
LLC	323	696	430	927	464,074

In fact was less frequent in the ICE–GB than in the London–Lund Corpus (LLC). On the other hand, *actually* was more frequent in the ICE–GB. This may suggest that *actually* is becoming more frequent and has developed additional functions over time. (The difference is statistically significant at p<0.0001 level) However the different frequencies may also reflect the greater formality of the conversations recorded in the LLC.

3.4 *In fact*

3.4.1 Introduction

In fact occurred in all text types and in both speech and writing. It was above all found in speech (80%). It was infrequent in highly interactive text types or activities compared with public dialogue. It was less frequent in telephone conversations (244 examples per 1,000,000 words) than in face-to-face conversation (367 examples per 1,000,000 words). We can make a comparison with *actually* which is characterised by a high frequency in telephone conversation (Table 3.3).

The lowest frequency was in broadcast talks, a type of scripted monologue. On the other hand, *in fact* was common in legal cross-examinations, demonstrations and unscripted speeches. In the written part of the corpus *in fact* was frequent in business letters and in popular writing, especially in the natural sciences (but the figures are low compared with speech).

In conversation *in fact* was found in 68 examples. The description of its formal and functional features and the interaction with the context will take conversation as the starting-point although it was less typical here than in other spoken text types.

3.4.2 Formal factors

We must describe the form and function of pragmatic markers and how they are related. The formal factors constraining the usage of *in fact* are for instance the grammatical context (whether the marker is found in a declarative sentence or an interrogative sentence), the position of the marker in the turn and in the sequential structure of the discourse, prosody, the elements with which it combines. In direct face-to-face conversation *in fact* was mainly used in declaratives. Two examples only were interrogative sentences. Compare:

   (1)   What What age were you when he went <u>in fact</u>
         (S1–076 065 FACE CONVERSATION)

In fact is added as an afterthought with a softening function (cf. Section 3.5.4). On the other hand, *in fact* in questions was particularly frequent in legal cross-examinations with a specialised use (see Section 3.6.1).

3.4.2.1 Position

Position is s specific to the text type and serves as a constraint on the interpretation along with other linguistic factors. Table 3.7 shows the position of *in fact* in conversation in the ICE-GB. *In fact* was most frequent in initial position (43 examples; 10 examples were also turn-initial). It also occurred medially and in end position.

Table 3.7 *In fact* in different positions in the utterance in conversation

Position	Frequency	Per cent
Initially *	43	63.2%
Medially	11	16.2%
End	14	20.6%
Total	68	100%

* Includes, for example, *but in fact, so in fact, and in fact, which in fact, because in fact*

A comparison with Oh's data from the American Switchboard corpus (telephone conversations) confirms the high frequency of initial position in conversation. A difference is the high frequency of end position in my data (see Table 3.8).

Table 3.8 The position of *in fact* in the ICE-GB and in the Switchboard corpus (Oh 2000)

Position	ICE-GB	Oh (2000)
Initial	63.2%	86%
Medial	16.2%	6%
End	20.6%	8%
Total	100%	100%

The high number of examples of *in fact* in initial position is noteworthy and has been associated with the function as a discourse marker. Compare Schwenter and Traugott, 'Syntactically it is a DM [discourse marker K.A.] occupying a clause-initial slot (often after *and*), but sometimes occurring clause-medially (typically in co-ordinating constructions, and in conversation, clause-finally' (Schwenter and Traugott 2000: 12). Oh, on the other hand, did not find that position had an effect on the function of *in fact*. According to Oh, '*[i]n fact* in medial position is used in the same way as it is used in initial position: that is, it marks an increase in the strength of a prior statement or assertion' (Oh 2000: 252). On *in fact* in end position see Section 3.5.4.

3.4.2.2 Prosodic factors

In fact can be both stressed and unstressed. In ICE-GB the number of unstressed examples was slightly higher than the examples with stress.[4] Traugott and Dasher (2002: 158) suggest that stress may distinguish between different meanings of *in fact*: 'however, impressionistically, the elaborative use . . . (*in fact₃*) can be relatively unstressed, whereas the adversative use (*in fact₂*) cannot'. In many examples it was difficult to determine

Table 3.9 Distribution of *in fact* according to whether it is stressed or unstressed

	Frequency	Per cent
Unstressed	29	42.6%
Stressed	17	25%
Indeterminate	22	32.4%
Total	68	100%

whether *in fact* was stressed or not (see Table 3.9). In addition to stress, pronunciation may be a clue to its function. In the elaborative use *in fact* is reduced and pronounced as [fæk].

Moreover *in fact* occurred with unfilled or filled pauses (usually before *in fact*) in 13 examples (Table 3.10).

Table 3.10 Distribution of *in fact* with pauses (conversation only)

	Pause before	Pause after	Total
Unfilled pause	4	2	6
Filled pause (*uh,uhm*)	4	3	7
Total	8	5	13

In fact occurred less often separated by a pause (or a tone unit boundary) than other frequent pragmatic markers. According to Altenberg (1987: 87), '*in fact* [in the London-Lund Corpus] was less frequently separated from the rest of the sentence than both *now* and *well* – the so-called "discourse marker use"' (cf. also Taglicht 2001).[5]

3.4.2.3 *In fact* and collocation

Pragmatic markers can have a vague interpretation. Collocations are therefore important clues to the distribution and strength of their meanings (Mortier and Degand 2009: 359). *In fact* (in conversation) co-occurred with *but* (4 examples) *and* (2 examples), *so* (2 examples), *because* (2 examples), *yes* (1 example).

3.5 *In fact* and function

In fact is flexible and has a meaning potential accounting for the meanings and functions it can have in the speech situation. However, both the choice of core meaning and the number of core meanings are open to discussion. It is generally recognised that *in fact* (and *actually*) is concerned with 'opposition' (or adversativity; Schwenter and Traugott 2000). Similarly, Fraser and Malamud-Makowski (1996) describe *in fact* (and related markers) as contrastive markers. However contrast or opposition is a complex notion which can be more or less strong and can be problematised in different ways. Another core meaning which has been suggested is deviation. According to Mortier and Degand (2009: 342), "it has been noted for *en fait* that the core meaning is not one of strict 'opposition' but rather one of deviation between p and q, i.e. accommodating for a sense of vagueness in the oppositive force" (Rossari 1992).

In fact (like *en fait*) can also refer to factuality (or truth). According to Mortier and Degand, factuality is a 'complex and contradictory value' integrated in the semantics of *in fact* which can explain how it is used in argumentation (Mortier and Degand 2009: 353). Mortier and Degand (2009: ibid.) claim that 'it often seems to be the function of *en fait* and *eigenlijk* to express that a seemingly subjective statement ("q") is the subjective truth, at least in the speaker's mind'. Moreover, adversativity and expectation are closely related. Oh (2000: 243), for example, claims that *actually* and *in fact* have a common core meaning namely 'unexpectedness'. For example, when *in fact* is used for opposition (contradiction, correction) we need to consider what the speaker assumes about the hearer's expectations. See the discussion of counter-expectation in Section 3.11.4.

Mortier and Degand (2009: 351) ended up by postulating three different meanings for the analysis of their written comparable data (*en fait* and *eigenlijk*): factuality, opposition and reformulation ('deviation'). In studies focusing on the grammaticalisation of *in fact* it has been common to distinguish two different meanings or 'core aspects' of *in fact* (the epistemic adverb *in fact₂* and a 'rhetorical-scalar' *in fact₃*) (Schwenter and Traugott 2000: 15).[6] In Schwenter and Traugott's analysis these core meanings correspond to the meanings of *in fact* (and *actually*) at different stages of the grammaticalisation process. *In fact₂* 'combines aspects of the meaning of strongly epistemic adverbs like *certainly* and adversative adverbs like *however*' (Schwenter and Traugott 2000: 11). *In fact₃* with rhetorical-scalar (or textual) function is a newcomer and belongs to the lexical domain of additivity (*and in fact*). Schwenter and Traugott (2000: 21) describe the use of *in fact₃* as follows: 'Speakers employ *in fact* not to rank q as opposed to or more consistent with the "facts" than p, but to rank q as a stronger rhetorical argument than p, which is nevertheless parallel in orientation to p.'

However both 'adversative' and 'elaborative' have been poorly described. Moreover, Schwenter and Traugott (2000) do not deal with sub-senses and less conventionalised functions but focus on the core functions associated with *in fact₂* and *in fact₃*, that is, a fairly coarse sub-classification. Mortier and Degand (2009), on the other hand, introduce a large number of sub-senses and implicatures both when the marker is adversative and when it is used for elaboration (what Mortier and Degand refer to as reformulation). *In fact* and *actually* have also developed functions which are characteristic of informal conversation. The discussion below will use the adversative and elaborative core meanings as a starting-point and discuss sub-senses and specialised uses associated with conversation and with other types of spoken language.

3.5.1 The adversative *in fact*

3.5.1.1 Emphasising reality

In fact can have the function of emphasising reality. However the emphasis is not on the 'reality' of the thing asserted but on the illocutionary force or truthfulness of what is asserted ('expressing that something is the truth'; cf. Bruti 1999). In Oh's (2000) analysis 'marking an increase in the strength of the assertion' is the only meaning of *in fact*. In (2) *in fact* enhances or emphasises the fact that if one writes down the conversation as a script (for research purposes) this will still only be what one can tell from memory. *In fact* typically collocates with *actually* (or with *really*).

(2) B: You're the only person who was there
So <,> you and yeah
and it's based on your memory <,>
<u>So even if</u> you write it down as
a script it's <u>still</u> only going to
be what you could <u>in fact actually</u> tell
(S1A-064 083–086 FACE)

3.5.1.2 Strong and weak opposition

The adversative meaning of *in fact* can be derived from the antithesis 'what appears to be the case – what is really the case' (cf. Mortier and Degand 2000 'truth-conditionality'). In the adversative meaning *in fact* has the function of connecting ideas or arguments. The adversative meaning is strongest and least controversial when *in fact* combines with *but* (5 examples in conversation). In (3), *(but) in fact* expresses or evokes 'explicit opposition' (cf. Mortier and Degand 2009: 356 'enhancement of an explicit opposition to p'):

(3) B: I was supposed to be going away
and then <,> phoned up <unclear-words> say he
was ill
so I stayed and I felt a bit
panicky about sort of <,> being on my
own all weekend
<u>But in fact</u> I had a really nice
time
(S1A-055 116–119 FACE)

The speaker had been afraid of being on her own all weekend but against expectations she had had a good time.

In fact can be adversative also if no opposition is expressed in ideational terms (in terms of the relationship between p and q). According to Mortier and Degand (2009: 354), 'In some cases, *eigenlijk* and *en fait* are the only markers yielding a linguistically expressed oppositive interpretation to an otherwise ideational opposition between *p* and *q*.' Example (4) illustrates the use of *in fact* to reject what has been said. Liquid nitrogen is first said to be the same price as milk. The speaker revises his earlier statement signalling this by means of *in fact*.

(4) B: Yes I always compare it
Liquid Uh liquid nitrogen is the s is
the same price as milk
<u>In fact</u> it's cheaper than milk and
uh liquid helium's about the same price
as uh wine
(S1A-088-090 FACE)

For the speakers in the conversation the interpretation of *in fact* seems to create little problem since the adversative value of *in fact* can be derived from the context. However, out of context such examples can create problems especially if prosodic information is not available.[7] Traugott and Dasher (2002: 158) discuss an example that they find ambiguous.

> Consider the rather artificial:
>
> Humanity is not often present. *In fact*, it/humanity is usually absent.
>
> Out of context, the written form *In fact, humanity is usually absent* is ambiguous: it could evoke either adversativity to or an elaboration of something that pre- ceded. In speech, *in fact* in both meanings may have a typical disjunct intonation with a sharp rise and fall; however, impressionistically, the elaborative use (*in fact$_3$*) can be relatively unstressed, whereas the adversative use (*in fact$_2$*) cannot.

In example (5) *in fact* has the pragmatic function of expressing what Mortier and Degand (2009) refer to as 'enhancement of an implicit opposition to p'. The speaker has been dis- cussing a grammar project with a colleague. Although one of the PhD students (Akiva) is going to work on the project the timescales may not (actually) be realistic (contrary to what the speaker had had in mind). The adversative meaning is further signalled by the rhetorical context suggested by the *if*-construction, *but basically* and *now it may well be the case*.

> (5) B: In fact Akiva if uh time permits may
>   also do some work on that as he
>   is interested in doing that for his P H D uh and it would be very
>   useful for the project if he did that
>   <u>But basically</u> this is the uh uh in my view the goal which we should be
>   moving towards <u>Now it may well be the case</u> that
>   the timescales I have in mind are not
>   <u>in fact</u> realistic and that we need to
>   get the sentence grammar reasonably correct first of
>   all cos that's
>   (S1A-024 094–096 FACE)

Implicit opposition is characteristic of the situation where speakers bring with them assumptions or expectations which are used in the interpretation process. According to Smith and Jucker (2000: 231): 'partners appear to bring with them a set of assumptions about what the other person will expect. As they converse, they apparently respond to those assumptions as well as to the information provided in the conversation itself'. In (6) the interpretation of the opposition expressed by *in fact* is helped by the presence of 'proved' which suggests that there may be competing claims. *In fact* conveys that there is some opposition with the implicit assumption or claim that one should always check that exams do not take place at the same time as a lecture.

> (6) A: Uhm so I check whether then whether the
>   students are doing their exam before after or

during my lecture which I never otherwise would
know until I arrived on Monday and uhm
<,> also <u>proving</u> at the point <u>the point</u>
<u>that</u> I have <u>in fact</u> thought about this
(S1A-082 046 FACE)

The lecturer wants to 'prove' that he has actually checked whether the students take their exam before his lecture. It is implied by the use of *in fact* that there may have been doubts about whether he has thought about this.

To sum up, the adversative *in fact* indicates that there is a contrast between what is apparent and what is real (a fact). The adversative meaning is strong only when *in fact* combines with *but*. In other examples *in fact* has implicit adversative meaning. When no opposition can be found *in fact* is used to emphasise reality (emphasise the illocutionary force associated with an assertion).

3.5.2 The elaborative *in fact*

In fact can also mean elaboration (cf. Mortier and Degand 2009 'deviation' or 'reformulation'). Elaboration is not subsumed under adversativity but is regarded as a separate core meaning since it does not have to do with the speaker's epistemic commitment or with opposition. The elaborative *in fact* is conceptually additive rather than oppositive. According to Schwenter and Traugott (2000: 21), 'the semantic/pragmatic function of *in fact₃* [the elaborative *in fact*] is not to rank q as opposed to or more consistent with the "facts" than p, but to rank q as a stronger rhetorical argument than p'.

The elaborative *in fact* is difficult to define formally (reflecting the fact that pragmatic markers are generally difficult to describe formally as a category). When *in fact* was initial in the clause it 'marks a change of posture' to a stronger claim (cf. Tognini-Bonelli 1993). However *in fact* can also be elaborative in medial position:

(7) A: I think they are in every tennis club
       I mean there's no tennis club doesn't
       have a kind of pecking order <,,> and
       the kind of you won't play with me
       cos I'm not good enough and that
       sort of team <,> rivalry and uh most
       intensely felt and seen by the ladies <,>
       <u>I mean There is in fact this lady</u>
       <u>I mean</u>
       ladies in groups are just phenomenally difficult <,>
       to cope with unless you get them and
       syphon them off into areas
       (S1A-081 035–040 FACE)

In fact has the elaborative function of clarification or precision (additionally marked by *I mean*) and lack of stress.

In fact elaborates on the previous utterance in different ways. In the majority of examples it is used to upgrade a claim (Smith and Jucker 2000: 214). When *in fact* is upgrading it can be seen 'as a form of stepping stone' from a preceding utterance to the following part of the discourse (Clift 2001: 256) providing the justification or warrant for a claim:

(8) A: But all I could remember you liked once
          was Kathy Acker and Jack Kerouac
          And I thought you might your taste might
          have changed
      B: I still like Jack Kerouac
          In fact I re-read most of them quite
          recently because you know Ape Ape my ex-boyfriend
      A: Yeah Uhm
      B: He got really into Jack Kerouac so I
          gave him a Jack Kerouac book when he
          went away <,>
          (S1A-015 237–243 FACE)

In fact is used by the speaker with the function to 'upgrade' the relevance of a previous statement (I still like Jack Kerouac) by adding that he has reread most of his books.

When *in fact* does not collocate with another pragmatic marker I have usually analysed it as upgrading:

(9) B: That's what I'm trying to say
          that you know all these things that Linda
          sets such great store by at the end
          of the day <,> don't add up to
          a row of beans In fact Heidi was saying to me yesterday
          how <,> uhm <,> the secretary of her
          <,> her ex-boss who was the president of
          of uhm part of M B C <,,> He rang her to tell Heidi that uhm
          he had died recently <,> and uh <,>
          her first reaction was to burst out laugh
          laughing <laugh>
          . . .

      But uhm <,,> but anyway I mean Linda gets off on this big business about you
      know sort of snob appeal <,> how clever all her acquaintances are and how
      wonderful they are in one way or other
      (S1A-010 245–249 . . . 278 FACE)

Linda has set great store on getting her O-levels and A-levels but such things do not 'add up to a row of beans'. The speaker supports her point about the non-importance of wordly things by adding what Heidi was saying yesterday about her ex-boss who was the President of a large company but had died recently. After this deviation the speaker returns to the topic of Linda.

However there are also examples where *in fact* is only loosely connected to the preceding utterance. This is the case in (10):

(10) B: This costs sixty-nine p and it's a hundred grammes
       What What's this
       A: Hundred grammes <unclear word> <,,>
       <u>In fact</u> the chocolate's almost identical isn't it
       It's uh fifty the Toblerone
       B: Oh there's so much stuff here
       (S1A-023 155–161 FACE)

The speakers are discussing the price of different types of chocolate. The chocolate they are looking at costs 'sixty-nine p', which is much more expensive than the Toblerone. We can visualise Speaker A considering the price and then concluding that the chocolate is almost identical to the other kind. Mortier and Degand (2009: 357) use the term 'mental leap' for 'a comment made by the speaker on a thought which is not or only implicitly expressed in the preceding context'. They found only few examples of this function in their written data (and only with *eigenlijk*). However, we can expect this function to be more frequent in conversation where it marks a 'topical shift'.

The elaborative *in fact* collocates with *and* rather than with *but* (adding details in a narrative). Speaker D has had her elbow rather than her (injured) wrist in plaster. The doctor was taking it very well that he had made a mistake.

(11) D: It wasn't up here at all <,>
       As he took the plaster off I mean
       it was agonising
       I said I can't move my wrist
       <u>and in fact</u> he saw me and was
       very good about m m my saying my
       wrist elbow's all right
       (S1A-022 209–212 FACE)

Mortier and Degand (2009) associated French *en fait* and Dutch *eigenlijk* with causality when it co-occurred with a marker with causal meaning. When *in fact* was found together with *so* (*so in fact*) I have followed Mortier and Degand and regarded it as causal:

(12) C: It'll be behind won't it
       B: Well no because you can choose the the
       material to match the bed clothes
       that's what I'm saying
       A: <u>So in fact</u> when you talk about not
       having too many flowers around you're going
       to have something like that in reverse
       (S1A-086 078–081 FACE)

The speakers are discussing whether they should choose curtains for the bedroom which have flowers on them. *So in fact* makes explicit that the function is causal (taking into account the consequences).

In fact together with *particularly* focuses on what comes next:

(13) B: Usually <,> <u>in fact particularly</u> in the evenings sort of <,>
      There isn't very much else to do <,,>
      and they are much less busy than during
      the day
      (S1A-059 193–94 FACE)

To sum up, the exact meaning of the elaborative *in fact* in conversation was difficult
to pin down. According to Lewis (2006: 17), 'there are few constraints on the use of
Elaborative *in fact;* it is compatible with a wide range of contexts, and in present-day
British English it is extending beyond elaboration'. The elaborative meaning is upgrading and strengthening. *In fact* can also have sub-senses such as precision (*I mean*),
adding details (*and in fact*) particularising (*particularly*), conclusion or adding consequences (*so in fact*). There were also meanings which I have characterised as a 'mental
leap'.

3.5.3 *In fact* as a hedging device

In informal conversation *in fact* may have functions which are not found in writing or in
more formal speech. These may be regarded as secondary effects (Mortier and Degand
2009: 355) or as situation-specific meanings. In (14) *in fact* is used to downtone the force
of the assertion 'by hinting at the possibility of an opposing view, thus contributing to the
management of face needs' (Beeching 2010: 152).

(14) <u>Well</u> I <u>uhm in fact</u> multiplied <u>uh</u> then to the two by ten to the two and got ten to
      the uh four but forgot that I had uh created twenty-five
      (S1A-24 033 FACE)

In fact would still be weakly adversative. However, the opposition is hinted at only: I must
concede that I in fact multiplied the two by ten, but forgot that I had created twenty-five.
In fact is used together with hesitation phenomena (*well, uh, uhm*) suggesting that the
speaker uses *in fact* with a weaker or softening force.

The downtoning function of *in fact* is suggested by the collocation *(yes uh in fact)* and
by the softening *actually*:

(15) A: Oh we had a long discussion about it on one occasion <,>
      B: Oh
      A: <u>Yes uh in fact</u> there's a there's a tendency towards the nice actually about
      your mother
      (S1A-023 073–075 FACE)

Example (16) contains many features characteristic of informal conversation (pauses,
repetitions, other pragmatic markers such as *sort of*). *In fact* is not strengthening but tones
down the meaning and is polite. The speaker is thinking of using the Comprehensive
Grammar as a model of grammar giving statements on what sort of syntactic structures
are permissible and which ones are frequently used.

(16) A: What sort of model are you thinking of
　　 B: <u>Well I I'm thinking</u> basically of a
　　 subset of the Comprehensive Grammar that <u>sort of</u>
　　 statement on what <u>sort of uh</u> syntactical <u>uh</u>
　　 structures are <u>in fact</u> uh permissible within that
　　 uh domain and which ones are uh frequently
　　 used which ones create cognitive processing problems which
　　 ones are easily processed
　　 (S1A-024 140–141 FACE)

To sum up, *in fact* is not only used emphatically to strengthen an assertion. In informal conversation, it can also have the opposite effect – namely to downtone the force of what is said.

3.5.4 *In fact* as a softener in end position

In conversation *in fact* sometimes had a softening function (mainly in end position). According to Traugott and Dasher (2002: 173), '[A]nother way in which *in fact* and *actually* are similar is that both may be used in spoken language to serve as hedges or softeners, though as one might expect from the fact that *actually* is the weaker of the two, it is more likely to be used this way.' *In fact* as a softener is associated with precision rather than opposition. There were 14 examples of final *in fact* all of which have been analysed as 'softeners' (6 examples stressed, 3 examples unstressed, 5 examples indeterminate). In the following example *in fact* is hedging or softening rather than adversative and strengthening. The nice young chap turned out not to be her boyfriend but a student in word studies.

(17) B: All right
　　 She says he's a a really nice
　　 young chap <,,>
　　 Well he's not really her boyfriend he's a uh
　　 he's a student in word studies <u>in fact</u> <,>
　　 C: Is he
　　 (S1A-090 145–149 FACE)

The use of *in fact* in end position is characteristic of conversation rather than of other text types. The main function of *in fact* is to establish and maintain a harmonious relationship between the speakers.

3.5.5 Summarising *in fact* in conversation

Table 3.11 shows the different frequencies of *in fact* in informal conversation.

Table 3.11 *In fact* in different functions in informal conversation

Adversative	
Emphasising reality	9
Explicit or implicit opposition	8
Elaboration	
Upgrading	14
Elaboration (and in fact)	6
Causal (so in fact)	4
Particularising (in fact particularly)	1
Precision (I mean in fact)	1
Topic shift (mental leap)	2
Conversation-specific uses (politeness)	
Softening (what has just been said)	16
Downtoning	3
Not classified	4
Total	68

In the adversative meaning (contrasting reality and appearance) *in fact* has the meaning 'emphasising reality' or strong and weak opposition. Explicit opposition is avoided. However, speakers may use *in fact* also when the opposition is only implicit. In addition, *in fact* had functions characteristic of politeness such as downtoning or softening an opinion with only an adversative 'note'.

The large number of *in fact* with elaborative as opposed to adversative function is striking (see Table 3.12). This suggests that this function fulfils important needs in conversation. There is little time for planning but speakers have to make continuous adjustments or corrections depending on the assessment of what goes on in conversation and the hearer's reactions.

Table 3.12 Distribution of *in fact* on different functions the ICE-GB

	Number	Per cent
Adversative (including emphasising reality)	17	25%
Elaborative (including downtoning and softening)	47	69.1%
Not classified	4	5.9%
Total	68	100%

3.6 *In fact* in public dialogue

In fact was significantly more frequent in public dialogue than in private dialogue (at $p<.001$) (see Table 3.13).

Table 3.13 The frequencies of *in fact* in private and public dialogue

	Frequency	Per 1,000,000	Number of words
Private dialogue	73	355	205,357
Public dialogue	110	643	171,062
Total	183	998	376,419

In fact was common in legal cross-examinations, demonstrations and unscripted speeches. It is associated 'with what Macaulay calls the "the language of authority": with assertive language used by middle (and upper) class speakers' (Schwenter and Traugott 2000: 11).

Legal cross-examination was the only category where *in fact* was more frequent than *actually* which suggests that it has some style-specific features in that text type (Section 3.6.1). I will also analyse *in fact* in broadcast discussion (3.6.2). Broadcast discussion represents an argumentative context where *in fact* can be expected to have different functions than in 'friendly' conversation.

3.6.1 *In fact* in legal cross-examinations

In fact occurs in different positions in the utterance in cross-examinations but with a different distribution than in face-to-face conversation. See Table 3.14.

Table 3.14 The distribution of *in fact* in cross-examinations compared with face-to-face conversation

	Cross-examinations		Face-to-face conversation
Initial position	11*	34.4%	63.2%
Medial position	18**	56.2%	16.2%
End position	3	9.4%	20.6%
Total	32	100%	100%

* 7 of the examples were introduced by another word
** 11 of the examples had a form of *be* before *in fact*

In fact was most frequent in medial position in cross-examinations (56.2%) and is therefore about four times as frequent as in conversation (16.2%) in that position. The number of examples in end position was much lower than in conversation. We can also note that *in fact* co-occurred with *and* (4 examples), *but, so, yes, uhm.*[8]

The frequent use of *in fact* can be explained by the structure and goal of the cross-examination and the roles of the examiner (defence counsel) and defendant (plaintiff). A cross-examination, unlike a conversation, is a highly structured event where questions and answers play an important role. Questions are used strategically and in a certain order by the defence counsel to build up an argument which will lead to a particular conclusion (for example, to show that the plaintiff's claims are not valid). Levinson (1979: 381) discusses the use of questions in cross-examinations with a witness in a rape case: 'the functions of questions here are to extract from the witness answers that build up to form a "natural" argument for the jury'.

In fact is generally assertive (i.e. it is used in a declarative sentence committing the speaker to the truth of what said). However, in the cross-examination it was also found in questions. It was, for instance, used to mark the transition to a question by the counsel where the answer to the question is already known.

In fact was used by the plaintiff's counsel (speaker A) in 18 examples. 10 of these examples were questions. The person interrogated (the plaintiff or a witness) used *in fact* in 13 examples (usually in the answer to the counsel's questions).[9] In (18), the plaintiff's counsel asks a question with the 'assertive' *in fact* in order to get an answer which will show the facts in the desired light. The plaintiff's response is 'yes indeed'.

(18) A: Did you <unclear words> these two businesses which are merged and that is
      <u>in fact</u> what you went through with me
      B> Yes indeed
      (S1B-065 032 CROSS-EXAMINATION)

By means of *in fact* the counsel can indicate the direction he wants the interrogation to take. The question is supposed to be answered by *yes* as is the case in the example above. According to Levinson (1979: 383), 'the questioner hopes to elicit a response that will count as part of an implicit argument.' In (18) it is implied that the witness knew about the merging of the two businesses. The motive for asking the question is to establish 'what the facts are' not to get information. Just like 'exam questions' in the classroom the questions are asked for a special purpose.

In the next example Person B (the plaintiff) claims compensation for an injury she received when climbing out of the pool which had a broken step. A (the plaintiff's counsel) addresses questions to the plaintiff with the sole purpose of displaying to the audience and to the judge what the facts are. The expected answer is acceptance (*yeah that's right*).

(19) A: Now you told My Lord that uh at first you didn't realise you'd cut yourself
      at all
      B: No I didn't <,,>
      A: <u>And the only reason</u> you were getting out of the pool was <u>in fact</u> to go and get
      a replacement cigarette
      B: Yeah that's right
      (S1B-066 019–021 CROSS EXAMINATION)

A question generally conveys that there is a lack of clarity about the facts. However, the strategy behind the counsel's question is to establish what the facts are in order to build up an argument leading to a conclusion.

In example (20) the counsel's intention is to establish (without any doubt) whether the plaintiff went down to another step or to the bottom (a fact which influences the plaintiff's claim for compensation for injuries inflicted by a broken step in the pool).

(20) A: At any rate di did you uhm g
      go down to another step or did you

> in fact uhm <,,> go to the bottom
> do you say
> B: Uhm <,,> my feet touched what I presume
> was either a step down or the bottom
> (S1B-066 012–013 CROSS EXAMINATION)

In (21) the context is argumentative (*but in fact*). The plaintiff (B) is a businessman being cross-examined by A (the defence counsel). B claims that the Midland Bank had been willing to lend him money although his business was going badly given their connection with Mr Sainsbury. *But in fact* makes the question challenging and accusing:

(21) B: Given their connection with Mr Sainsbury and I'd
          understood they'd had very satisfactory re
          uh relationship with Mr Sainsbury uhm <,> I
          don't see that the Midland Bank would've
          had any problem <,,>
       A: <u>But in fact</u> in the case of the
          Midland Bank <unclear-words>
          <u>You didn't know about that</u>
       B: I was not aware of that no sir
          (S1B-061 059–061 CROSS EXAMINATION)

In (22) A is the high court judge accusing the witness of saying that 'he can't see' when in fact he can.

(22) A: That I can understand very readily <,>
          It's the idea that you start off
          consciously <,> deliberately <,> <u>saying I can't see</u>
          <u>when in fact you can</u> and you know
          you can and you then somehow <,> persuade
          yourself into a state of actual blindness
          (S1B-070 124–125 CROSS EXAMINATION)

It is possible that the frequent use of *in fact* in cross-examination in comparison with conversation should be described as 'overuse'. The truth of what has been said is asserted even without *in fact*. However, *in fact* has an important role in establishing the speaker's professional identity and control over the proceedings. In particular, *in fact* has the role of organising the cross-examination as a series of events (or arguments) leading to a conclusion. *And in fact* marks the transition to an argument according to the agenda for a cross-examination:

(23) A: And did he make it clear that he
          wasn't putting in any money
       B: No Sir He took away all the uh pieces of
          information which we gave him uhm
          <u>And in fact</u> we were subsequently for informed

> afterwards by him that uh they wouldn't be
> willing to lend us the money
> (S1B-061 021–024 CROSS EXAMINATION)

And in fact adds some information making it clearer that the bank was not willing to lend the money.

Both the counsel and the defendant use *in fact*. This can be explained by its close association with truth, factuality and objectivity. In (24) the conflict has to do with a contract. The plaintiff (B) claims that he was not aware that it was necessary to come up with money in order to get the disputed contract. *In fact* co-occurs with *but*, negation and *actually*. It is repeated in order to strengthen the plaintiff's point:

(24) A: Did you know that Ward had secured the property had got the contract
      B: I was not aware of anything other than the original meeting There were some
         conversations with Mr Sainsbury popping in and out of our premises urging us
         to arrange finance and I informed him that it was already under way with A S
         C consultants
         But I was not aware that there was a need to actually come up with any money I
         am not aware until <u>in fact</u> this court hearing that there was <u>in fact</u> a deposit paid
         in December <,>
         (S1B-061 108–113 CROSS-EXAMINATION)

In (25) the plaintiff had asked for three years' accounts before taking over the company which is what they got. *I believe . . . in fact . . . eventually* ... adds a tone of finality to the speaker's argument:

(25) A: If you were going to take over a
         company you would want to see how it
         had fared over a number of years wouldn't you
      B: We asked for three years' accounts
         <u>I believe</u> that that is what <u>in fact</u>
         we <u>eventually</u> got
         (S1B-065 132–134 CROSS EXAMINATION)

In fact adds a 'factual' note. This is illustrated in (26). Speaker D, who has been called as a witness for the prosecution, modifies (clarifies, reformulates) a question by referring to what is clearer, more correct and 'true' in the clause introduced by *in fact* (in fact we know there was a rupture don't we):

(26) D: I'll put it a bit more clearly
         <unclear-words> observation
         The question <u>wasn't very clearly</u> phrased
         <u>Uhm in fact</u> we know that there was
         a rupture <u>don't we</u> of the ligament <,>
         Now it is very unusual isn't it to
         get a rupture of the ligament as a

> result of a mere forward action of the
> head <,,>
> (S1B-068 139–142 CROSS EXAMINATION)

(27) is another example of the argumentative function of *in fact* in the cross-examination. *In fact* refers to something considered to be an 'objective' fact rather than an opinion (the repairs were in hand) and thus supporting the speaker's claim (I know that I did not want to leave the construction site open over night):

(27) B: <u>I know</u> that I did I did <u>not</u>
         want to leave it open over night
         <u>In fact</u> the repairs were already in hand
         (S1B-069 162–163 CROSS EXAMINATION)

In fact has text-specific or specialised functions in the cross-examination which can be related to the description of the social situation. The 'actors' are typically a counsel or a judge asking questions and a defendant or plaintiff answering the questions. The question-answer exchanges make up the backbone of the cross-examination and are oriented to a specific goal, namely to establish what took place and the order of the events. The speakers exploit the meaning 'factuality' or 'truth' in complex and contradictory ways (a point made by Mortier and Degand 2009: 353). *In fact* is typically used by the examiner to 'prove' that the plaintiff was right or wrong by referring to facts and not for persuasion. *In fact* was, for instance, used in questions by the plaintiff's counsel where the answer to the question is already known to both the counsel and the plaintiff. However as we have seen, in a cross-examination both the counsel and the plaintiff claim to possess the truth.

It follows that *in fact* in cross-examinations is multifunctional. It has meanings such as truth (or factuality), use in questions, power or authority, indexing social role as counsel or examiner. It can be used as a 'contextualization cue' by the counsel to control the argumentation in the courtroom. However, we need to distinguish between meaning (sub-senses) and function. *In fact* is polysemous with sub-senses which are adversative or elaborative. In addition it can have a number of contextual functions (including indexical stance meanings associated with power or politeness) emerging in actual use.

The use of *in fact* in cross-examinations can also be compared with its function in debates. Biber and Finegan (1989: 114) give examples of *in fact* from a parliamentary debate and comment that the use of 'stance features' such as *in fact* or *actually* seems to convey a persuasive force. In Section 3.6.2, I consider the use of *in fact* in broadcast discussion.

3.6.2 *In fact* in broadcast discussion

A broadcast discussion follows special rules and conventions. There is a moderator or a 'host' inviting speakers to take the floor, determining how long every speaker is allowed to talk, organising speaker change, etc. The topic is controversial and a certain amount of disagreement is expected. Moreover, the topic is determined beforehand and the participants have therefore had the opportunity to prepare their arguments.

In fact was frequent in initial position (15 examples) which can be associated with the 'monological' character of the debate. However, it was less frequent in initial position than in conversation and it was unusual in end position (2 examples) (see Table 3.15).

Table 3.15 The distribution of *in fact* in broadcast discussion compared with face-to-face conversation

	Broadcast discussion		Face-to-face conversation
Initial position	15	48%	63.2%
Medial position	14	45%	16.2%
End position	2	7%	20.6%
Total	31	100%	100%

In fact in the broadcast discussion takes one 'into the intricacies of interaction' (Haviland 1989: 36). According to Haviland (1987: 343) categories of evidence and truth can have a fighting rhetorical role, especially if the context is argumentative.

> [w]e often fight with truth, and the basic techniques of contentiousness are often inseparable from the same matters that are routinely encoded in the grammatical category of evidence, truth, reliability, knowledge and authority—relative to the context of the speech event.

The functions of *in fact* are related to the goals of the broadcast discussion (to win by having the best arguments). We can make a comparison with *in fact* in cross-examinations where truth is presupposed and not fought about.

Example (28) is from a broadcast discussion where the participants discuss a tax on property which depends on a division of the population into different (income) bands. Speaker I argues that this tax will be easier to administrate since it is progressive. *In fact* is used in a series *but, obviously, certainly, so, in fact, actually, in fact, in fact* with persuasive force.

(28) I: I don't think it's an imbalance
      But you're going to obviously find
      uhm with this tax that the way it's
      going to operate it's going to
      be a lot easier to collect certainly a
      lot cheaper to administrate
      So when you're in fact looking at
      the bands of property you 're going to
      actually see that the one in band A
      is in fact paying two thirds less than
      the person in the centre band and the
      person in the high band that uh Margaret
      is referring to is in fact paying two
      and a half times the person in the
      lowest band
      (S1B-034 076–077 BROADCAST DISCUSSION)

In example (29) *I think in fact* signals the speaker's personal conviction keyed against a normative view-point 'what other people think' (with regard to the issue whether there should be one national police force). The participants are discussing whether the financing of the police should be transferred to the regions or come from the central government. *I think in fact* is used to distinguish the speaker's position from that of other possible positions on an issue where opinions are divided.

(29)   E: I don't agree with the view which was
expressed by Sir John Wheeler that because at
present ninety per cent of the financing of
the police comes from central government something like
ninety per cent of the control should be
at the centre
I think in fact you should certainly transfer
funding to the regions along the lines that
Roy Hattersley perhaps has in mind but that
you should go further and recognise that it
is in the local community that most of
the public is going to be aware of
the functioning of the police and wishes to
see proper accountability exercised
(S1B-033 039–040 BROADCAST DISCUSSION)

Example (30) is from a political discussion (on the topic of whether British troops should enter Iraqi territory). *In fact* is used for persuasion and not for emphatic certainty. As in the previous example *in fact* occurs together with other persuasive markers: *certainly, actually, in fact, I think, the fact is, indeed.*

(30)   A: Kenneth Clarke
B: N N No it certainly does not as
uhm as Paddy's just said and
actually <,> normally I'd be amazed by
the unanimity In fact on such a serious occasion I
think it's quite impressive
Uh the the the fact is that it
must be right for our troops to go
into Iraqi territory
Indeed they're flying over it and attacking
Iraqi targets in Iraqi territory now because there's
on no other way of removing an
army from Kuwait
(S1B-027 091–095 BROADCAST DISCUSSION)

In (31) *in fact* is used in a more subtle way. The issue discussed is whether country life is a myth or reality. Sir Simon Gourlay and Rodney Legge are participants in the debate. The speaker masks the disagreement as agreement by means of *in fact* (would you not agree

Rodney Legge that nature is 'in fact' the creation of man). *In fact* makes it more difficult for the opponent to disagree:

> (31)   A: I mean again Sir Simon Gourlay you talk about the countryside as the farmer's workshop and workplace and actually <,> nature would you not agree Rodney Legge is <u>in fact</u> the creation of man
> (S1B–037 036 BROADCAST DISCUSSION)

In broadcast discussion *in fact* (typically in combination with *I think*) is used by the participants with the specialised function of taking up a position to other positions or to 'a normative viewpoint', that is what people say or think. It can also be used for persuasion. The persuasive force is suggested by its co-occurrence with other markers such as *certainly, obviously,* etc.) pushing the argument in a certain direction. The factual meaning of *in fact* can also be used strategically 'to frame disagreement as agreement' (cf. Biber and Finegan 1989: 115).

3.7 *In fact* in monologues

In fact fulfils important functions both in demonstrations and in unscripted speeches, that is, in types of monologic discourse.

3.7.1 *In fact* in demonstrations

A demonstration is an example of a monologue. It is similar to unscripted speeches in being unprepared although (in both cases) the speaker may base his or her speech on notes. As in other discourse types *in fact* is positionally versatile. See Table 3.16.

Table 3.16 The distribution of *in fact* in different positions in demonstrations

	Demonstration		Face-to-face conversation
Initial position	10*	34.5%	63.2%
Medial position	18*	62.1%	16.2%
End position	1	3.4%	20.6%
Total	29[10]	100%	100%

*Including *and in fact, but in fact* (2 examples), (*and*) so *in fact* and *which in fact, so (whereas) . . . in fact* (2), *well . . . in fact, and . . . in fact* (5 examples), *and therefore . . . in fact*

In fact in demonstrations was placed in medial position in more than half of the examples. End position was unusual.

As in cross-examinations or broadcast discussions *in fact* has special uses. An example of a demonstration in the corpus would be a lecture where the speaker's goal is to explain or demonstrate something to an audience.

The context is causal (cause-effect) rather than adversative. However, *in fact* can be used 'with an adversative note' (Mortier and Degand 2009: 355) or implicature to suggest that there is a conflict with previous expectations or with predictions made on the basis of earlier experiments.

(32) A: If you get something swimming in the medium
      then it won't <,,>
      Since they contain chlorophyll you can <u>in fact</u>
      change your optics to fluorescence
      And actually the chloroplast shines up in that
      way <,,>
      (S2A-051 081–083 DEMONSTRATION)

In (33) the causal context is flagged by *so whereas*. The lecturer explains what is remarkable about the new microscope: by using a stronger microscope we can now see things which do not have this filter.

(33) A: <u>So whereas</u> intrinsically we know we can only
      uhm <,> see in the microscope things down
      to point two five microns in reality we
      <u>can in fact</u> now go to an order
      of magnitude below that <,,>
      (S2A-051 024 DEMONSTRATION)

The lecture from which example (34) is extracted takes place at the university and deals with the representation of caricatures and satires in art. The lecturer has explained how not only physiognomies but also dress are used for caricaturing people from different social classes.

(34) now you've got no uh physiognomies uh physiognomies are always distorted but
      you notice that dress is often used to signify different social class here uhm there
      you've got the fops gentleman uhm and there is a satire on an individual this time
      uhm <,> this is <u>in fact</u> a satire on the Earl of Burlington
      (S2A-057 043)

The lecturer could have said simply 'this is a satire on the Earl of Burlington'. However, without *in fact* the connection between discourse segments would be less clear. *In fact* emphasises that the satire on the Earl of Burlington can be predicted from what has just been said (distorted physiognomies, dress, etc.). Position does not seem to play a role when *in fact* is used in demonstrations, that is, in monologues. The speaker could also have said *In fact this is a satire on the Earl of Burlington* with the same meaning.

The next example has the same provenance (it is taken from the lecture on satire in imagery). *In fact* marks the utterance as an explanation. However, it also conveys an adversative note: 'it was erected in memory of the destruction of the city by the South Sea Islands (?) not by fire':

(35) You've got the Monument which is in effect a kind of takeoff of the uhm monu-
      ment to the Great Fire of London and this monument here was <u>in fact</u> erected
      in memory of the destruction of the city by the South Sea uh Islands <u>in fact</u> not
      by fire
      (S2A 57 012 DEMONSTRATION)

In *fact* refers to the consequences of having photo detectors to process images (so sensitive that they can process images). The frequency of *in fact* (and *actually*) in demonstrations is remarkable. *In fact* is inserted whenever the speaker wants to convey authority or expert knowledge:

(36) A: The only important thing that's happened is
that uh it's now possible to use
<u>such</u> a low light level <u>that</u> <u>in fact</u>
if you were to look down some microscopes
now you couldn't see an image that's
coming up simply <u>because</u> now you can have
photo detectors which are are <u>so</u> sensitive that
<u>in fact</u> they can receive the image and
process it even though when you look down
the tube you can't see it
(S2A-051 005 DEMONSTRATION)

In fact is causal rather than adversative (cf. also *because in fact, so in fact*).
Besides its use in explanations it can add a stronger or final argument:

(37) A: Uh the distinction that Mrs George makes is
between political and social satires
But of course it's you can't always
work it out as quite often the two
mingle
<u>In fact</u> one ways one of the ways
of getting a a good comic effect is
to combine the sort of fashion plate with
political caricature <,>
(S2A-057 023–025 DEMONSTRATION)

In fact adds support for the claim that political and social satire cannot always be distinguished.

To summarise, *in fact* has special functions in demonstrations. It is for instance typically used for explanations, for referring to consequences or for strengthening an argument. It involves elaboration (reformulation, rephrasing) rather than adversativity or factuality. *In fact* is also linked to a special speaker identity (lecturer) associated with expert knowledge and authority.

3.7.2 *In fact* in unscripted speeches

Unscripted speeches also represent one of the discourse types where *in fact* is frequent (after legal cross-examinations and demonstrations). They have in common with demonstrations, lectures and broadcast debates that the speaker addresses an audience. Although the speech is unscripted it has a particular topic and the speaker has a certain goal in mind (to present something in a convincing and interesting way). *In fact* occurred more often in initial position than in demonstrations but not as often as in face-to-face conversation (see Table 3.17).

Table 3.17 The distribution of *in fact* in different positions in unscripted speeches. A comparison is made with face-to-face conversation

	Unscripted speeches		Face-to-face conversation
Initial	25*	45.4%	63.2%
Medial	26	47.3%	16.2%
Final	4	7.3%	20.6%
Total	55	100%	100%

* After *and, well, but, so, cos, however, when*

Both in demonstrations and unscripted speeches *in fact* has special functions which depend on the relationship between the speaker (a lecturer) and the audience. In 7 examples *in fact* was used together with *but* which suggests that it is argumentative. However, there is not an opponent as in the broadcast discussion but the argument is directed against an implicit claim or a 'strawman'. In (38) the topic is Great Temples at the British Museum. The speaker establishes solidarity with the audience by referring to what 'most of us know'.

(38) A: Here we have Corinthian <,> which for my money always looks exactly like
Chinese cabbage misbehaving itself because that's the plant you see most often
<u>But in fact</u> uhm <u>most of us know</u> it's really a version of that huge robust plant
the acanthus <,> which many of you have in your gardens
(S2A-024 068–069 UNSCRIPTED SPEECHES)

In (39) the lecturer has mentioned several examples of great architecture which have impressed him because of the architect's imagination and wit. What is more, in such buildings windows may metamorphose into something different whether one twiddles around with them or not.

(39) A: But good architecture does not demand a stiff
upper lip a nervous twiddling about with window
sills <u>In fact</u> windows may metamorphose into something completely
different <u>anyway</u> <,>
(S2A-040 080–082 UNSCRIPTED SPEECHES)

12 examples contained *and in fact*. *And in fact* adds further details:

(40) A: And he he really was Kapp was really
a most charming man
<u>And</u> he was <u>in fact</u> the Pender Professor
for a few years when I first came
to U C L in May nineteen forty-six
and I was present at the retirement party

given to Kapp when somebody in one of
the speeches after the dinner said that in
fact Professor Kapp was the only professor in
the University of London who looked like a
professor <,,>
(S2A-041 023–025 UNSCRIPTED SPEECHES)

In (41) the topic is a lecture on 'the ancient Celts through Caesar's eyes'. The lecturer discusses the view held by some people that the Gauls were 'admirable noble savages' and gives as example the famous statue called the dying Gaul. However the dying Gaul does not represent a Gaul but is one of the Galatians of Turkey. *In fact* signals that the information is unexpected.

(41) A: This again is a a a view of
other peoples which uh is recurrent <,> through
history
Perhaps that is personified by this famous statue
called the dying Gaul <,> uh which you
can see on the Capitoline in Rome which
is a a Roman copy of a a
Hellenistic Greek original
In fact it doesn't show a Gaul of France
it shows one of the Galatians of Turkey
<,> distant cousins of the Gauls <,> uh
from a a a Greek victory monument after
one of the defeats of the Gauls
(S2A-022 059–062 UNSCRIPTED SPEECHES)

In fact is associated with adversativity and with counter-expectation. It can express solidarity with the audience (we both know something) or that something is unexpected.

3.8 *In fact* in writing

In fact is also found in writing although less frequently than in speech. The differences in frequency between text types are less striking than in speech since the number of examples are few. The frequency in business letters is however noteworthy since *in fact* is more frequent than *actually*. On the other hand, *in fact* did not occur at all in administrative or regulatory writing such as an information leaflet or library regulations. Business letters are distinguished from personal letters by their formality. In (42) the writer suggests that it would be an advantage if the (bank) statement is dispatched at the beginning instead of the middle of the month and underlines this with *in fact* (I see that your statement is in fact dispatched at the end of the month):

(42) I see that your statement is in fact despatched to you in the middle of the month
and it occurs to me that you might find it of assistance if this was dispatched to
you at the beginning of the month. (W16-016–019 BUSINESS LETTER)

In fact conveys formality. It co-occurs with a number of formal features such as the passive (*is despatched to you, if this was dispatched to you*), the use of subordinate clauses, abstract vocabulary (*dispatch*), complex constructions (*you might find it of assistance*). The use of *in fact* is adversative but polite (it is used to downtone a degree of opposition). It can indirectly be used to give some information about the type of text (it must be a business letter since it contains *in fact*).

3.9 Summarising *in fact*

The functional diversity of *in fact* supports the hypothesis that it is best regarded as having a meaning potential organised around several core functions. In its literal meaning *in fact* has to do with factuality and truth. However, its most prominent core meanings are adversativity and elaboration. Adversativity introduces a distinction between what is apparent and what is actual or real. The adversative meaning depends on supporting elements in the context such as the contrastive *but* (strong opposition). However, *in fact* can also have a weak adversative meaning which depends on the speaker's assumptions about what the hearer believes and expectations 'in the air'.

In conversation the adversative meaning was rare. However an adversative note can be perceived when *in fact* is used to downtone the assertion for face-saving purposes. *In fact* was above all used with elaborative sub-senses. The speaker used *in fact* to acknowledge the hearer's presence for example by rephrasing what has been said or upgrading its relevance.

Moreover, *in fact* has more specialised uses which are not sufficiently described as factual, adversative, elaborative or in terms of expectation. I have argued that the core meaning can be 'stretched' or exploited in different ways depending on features present in the communication situation. The 'new' functions of *in fact* depend on the social identity of the speaker, the speaker-hearer relationship and the goals of the activity. This has been illustrated with some social situations where *in fact* was frequent. *In fact* was, for instance, used in cross-examinations to mark the transition to a question where both the speaker and the hearer know the answer to the question. Broadcast discussions are by their nature 'fighting'. *In fact* was therefore used with persuasive rather than strengthening force. It could also be used to 'emphasise the speaker's position in the view of divergent opinions' (*I think in fact*). Demonstrations and unscripted speeches are similar in that there is not a single hearer but an audience. However, in demonstrations *in fact* was typically used for explanations, for referring to results or to strengthen an argument. In unscripted speeches it was used to argue against what is commonly thought. It could be used strategically to establish solidarity with the hearer (we both know what the facts are) or to refer to something as unexpected and therefore interesting.

3.10 *Actually*

3.10.1 Introduction

Actually has a different distribution from *in fact*. It was frequent in face-to-face conversation, telephone conversation and business transactions, that is in text types implying a high degree of interaction and involvement. In these text types it was more frequent than *in fact*. On the other hand, it was infrequent in debates and cross-examinations, that is in more argumentative text types. *Actually* is mainly dialogical. However, it was even more frequent than *in fact* in demonstrations and in unscripted speeches. In writing *actually* was most frequent in informal categories such as social letters and popular writing within the humanities and social sciences (Section 3.3).

Actually stands out because of its 'overuse' in some text types. The following example is from a telephone conversation:

> (43) A: There's nobody you want to seduce
>   B: I'm working on it Give me time <laugh> Uhm Oh yes there is <u>actually</u>
>   <u>Actually</u> I am <u>Actually</u> yes I've got my <unclear-words> I've got one on
>   the back burner <u>actually</u> I <unclear-syllable> Yes It just struck me
>   A: <u>Actually actually</u> <laugh> Oh yes Tell me more
>   (S1A-091 224–239 TELEPHONE CONVERSATION)

B is responding to A's question 'there's nobody you want to seduce'. Her answer contains several examples of *actually:* 'there is *actually* (someone I want to seduce), *actually* I am (working on it), I've got one (guy) on the back burner *actually*.' Speaker B's habit of using *actually* is also noted by Speaker A *(actually actually)* followed by laughter.

The multifunctionality and flexibility of *actually* have been much discussed but not with regard to the variation in different text types or in speech and writing (see for instance Tognini-Bonelli 1993; Lenk 1998; Smith and Jucker 2000; Clift 2001; Aijmer 2002; Mortier and Degand 2009[11]).

Actually has been discussed both alone and in comparison with *in fact* (cf. Oh 2000 and Section 3.2). It occurs more frequently in British than American data as shown by comparing its frequency in the ICE-GB corpus and the Santa Barbara Corpus. In the ICE-GB corpus *actually* occurred 166 times per 100,000 words to be compared with only 49 times per 100,000 words in the American data. Above all, *actually* has been discussed from the point of view of variation and change over time from the point of view of grammaticalisation and pragmaticalisation (Traugott and Dasher 2002 and Defour et al. 2010). We can also note that *actually* was more frequent in the ICE-GB Corpus than in the London-Lund Corpus which suggests that its popularity may be increasing (Section 3.3). However, in the present chapter the concern is with its variability contingent on the text type and situation especially in spoken language rather than with the time factor or the variety of English.

3.10.2 Formal factors

Actually (like *in* fact) does not have a single meaning but a meaning potential. We also need to consider other resources which are open to the speaker to express meaning such as prosody or collocation and position in the turn sequence or in the utterance. To begin with the formal properties of *actually* will be discussed focusing on their frequencies in conversation.

3.10.2.1 Position

Actually occurred 392 times in the data from direct conversation. A sample of 200 words has been used to investigate its grammatical and prosodic properties. *Actually* can be inserted into many different slots in the utterance (Table 3.18). The constraints therefore have to do with frequencies:

Table 3.18 *Actually* in different positions in the utterance in conversation

	Frequency	Per cent
Initially*	43	21.5%
Medially	113	56.5%
End	44	22%
Total	200	100%

* Preceded for example by *well, but, whereas, because*
Out of the 43 examples found in initial position 22 were also turn-initial

Medial position includes both (44) and (45):

(44) but I <u>actually</u> remember getting a whole series of uhm books that'd been in in a sort of bargain basement
(S1A 013 172 FACE)

(45) You know I mean it would seem to be squandering it to <,> <u>actually</u> eat it for one's own enjoyment (S1A 010 049 FACE)

Medial position was most frequent (56.5%). However the frequency is lower than in the sample from the BNC analysed by Defour et al. (2010: 169). According to Defour et al., *actually* occurred in medial position in 69.9% of the spoken data; only 8.8% of the examples of *actually* were found in initial position in their data compared with 21.5% in my data. However, the number of examples in final position was similar (21.6% in Defour et al.'s data and 22% in the ICE-GB sample). In Oh's data from telephone calls, in comparison, *actually* was less frequent in final position (8%) while the initial position was even more frequent than in my data (Oh 2000: 34%).

The position of *actually* is closely associated with other factors such as the distinction between speech and writing and between different text types. We can also make a comparison with *in fact*. See Table 3.19.

Table 3.19 *Actually* and *in fact* in different positions in the utterance in conversation

	In fact	Actually
Initially	63.2%	21.5%
Medially	16.2%	56.5%
End	20.6%	22%
Total	100%	100%

Actually was less frequent than *in fact* initially. It was above all found in medial position and it was slightly more frequent than *in fact* in final position.[12] According to Clift the syntactic flexibility of *actually* is 'exploited by interactional exigencies' (Clift 2001: 246). However, position is a complex phenomenon and the position of *actually* is also associated with functions such as hedging.

3.10.2.2 Prosodic factors

Actually was never followed by a pause in my sample data of 200 words from conversation. This suggests that it is integrated in the utterance. However, Taglicht (2001: 3) refers to *actually* as a 'marginal' element in the sentence from the point of view of syntactic-semantic structure. According to Taglicht (2001: 7), this also has consequences for its prosody. Intonationally *actually* is attached to the preceding not the following node. In this chapter I have not studied the prosody of *actually*. However, in an earlier study of *actually* on the basis of the London–Lund Corpus I found that it occurred with the tone mainly in final position (70% of the examples) but was less frequently stressed in medial (29%) or in initial position (34%) of the examples) (Aijmer 2002: 262).

3.10.2.3 *Actually* and collocation

It was shown in Section 3.5.1.2 that *in fact* has a weak meaning which could be made explicit in the vicinity of another marker such as *but*. What is noticeable in the ICE-GB data is the high number of *well* together with *actually* compared with other collocates. We can also note that *actually* had a large number of collocations with other pragmatic markers compared with *in fact* (see Table 3.20).

Table 3.20 *Actually* and collocations (face-to-face conversation only)*[13]

Well actually	15
And actually	9
Actually I think	6
Oh (no) actually	5
But actually	5
Actually sort of	5
Actually uh(m)	3
Actually I mean	3
Actually (quite) kind of	3
So actually	2
Actually really	2

* Occurring once: *no but actually, actually you know, actually I don't know, I think actually, because actually, whereas actually, just actually, actually probably*

In addition, *actually* co-occurred with filled pauses (*uh(m)*) in 2 examples and once with an unfilled pause.

Actually could also be a part of a cluster of pragmatic markers:

(46) A: <u>No I mean so actually you know</u> we're
        we're mainly I B M orientated
        (S1A-029 158–160 FACE)

3.11 *Actually* and function

I will be exploring the hypothesis that *actually* does not have a fixed meaning but a meaning potential, that is a rich semantic representation consisting of senses, sub-senses, implications, salient and non-salient meanings and connotations. However, the meaning potential must be organised in some way which explains how certain meanings are more general (conventionalised, salient) and others are less salient or specialised. *Actually* (like *in fact*) has a number of sub-senses which can be classified as adversative and elaborative. We also need to consider its literal meaning factuality (emphasising reality). Following Schwenter and Traugott (2000: 23) adversative and elaborative will be regarded as distinct polysemies (with a number of sub-senses). Moreover, *actually* has a number of specialised meanings which become relevant only in a particular social situation.

Actually was more frequent in face-to-face conversation than *in fact*. We can therefore expect it to have more functions which are specific to conversation and differ from those discussed for *in fact*.

Actually (like *in fact*) has to do with opposition. Opposition is, however, a complex notion and I will use the term adversativity as an umbrella term which includes functions where opposition is only implied or evoked and about counter-expectation.[14] *Actually* in conversation is associated with hedging and apologising. It can convey that something is unexpected, that it is surprising or newsworthy, or that is undesirable and problematic.

3.11.1 Emphasising reality

The original meaning 'actuality' (what is real or factual) is present in *actually* (like *in fact*). In (47) *actually* is closely related to what is 'really' or in fact the case (as indicated by its occurrence in the clause initiated by *as if*). It has been analysed as emphasis or emphasising reality.

(47) B: It's It's as if he's
hypnotising <,> as if his stillness and his
poise actually hypnotises the audience <,,>
(S1A-045 120 FACE)

Similarly in (48) the meaning component which is emphasised is actuality (what is really the case):

(48) B: Oh yes this is a really good idea <,>
You've actually got to find out what you're actually doing
(S1A 002 132–133 FACE)

3.11.2 Explicit and implicit opposition

But actually (9 examples) makes the opposition or contrast with a preceding proposition or assumption explicit. In the example below *but actually* 'corrects' an assumption which follows from what the speaker has just said (the wing is apart from the main house and is therefore less nice). It is claimed that although the wing is apart from the house it is still a lovely pile.

(49) B: We trooped down to the wing which is
actually apart
It's apart from the main house
But actually it's it's a lovely
pile It's right <,,> it's on a
sort of hill <,> and you've got
lovely views looking out to the South Downs
But unfortunately both Saturday and Sunday it was
really foggy
(S1A-036 155–159 FACE)

In (50) Speaker A has been collecting tapes to be used for the National Curriculum but changes his mind and is now collecting dialects for a start since 'a smashing selection' is available. (*But*) *actually* makes explicit the contrast (the speaker is no longer collecting tapes of spoken language):

(50) A: Yes <,>
We we've got we've got to
as far as the the National Curriculum is
concerned But actually at the moment we've got
a particularly <,> sort of smashing selection of
of dialects on tape <,>
So we're trying to
We're we we we're sort of
collecting those for a start
(S1A-012 006–010 FACE)

When *actually* was not preceded by *but* it can have the function of implicit opposition: the speaker uses it strategically to negotiate a claim which can be derived from the context only. In (51) Speaker B has not actually talked to his tutor before choosing a course although this may be expected.

(51) B: Uhm in clinical psychology sort of thing
Oh we've had lectures on it and
stuff
I <,> I haven't actually talked to my
individual tutors or anything <,>
A: Yeah
B: Probably worthwhile doing that I think you know
just to say <,> how do you think
I rate <,>
(S1A-035 084–088 FACE)

3.11.3 Hedging and politeness

With *actually* the contradiction expressed is mild. *Actually* (unlike *in fact*) can be associated with hedging and softening of the contradiction (Mortier and Degand 2009 refer to the 'non-oppositive effects' of contradiction). In (52) Speaker B contradicts A (it's not a small garden) underlining the contrast with the preceding utterance by means of *actually*. *Actually* is compatible with 'a partial or unimportant contradiction' (Hickey 1991: 371). According to Hickey, it 'plays down' the negative element in what is corrected'. The hearer may have had good reasons to think that the garden is quite big.

> (52) A: Whereabouts
>   Sh she's got a small garden <unclear-word>
>   the fire the bonfire and
>   B: <u>Actually</u> it's not a small garden
>   No it's not small it's quite
>   big <,>
>   (S1A-025 135–137 FACE)

Actually conveys an apologetic sense which can be additionally signalled by *well* and by *probably*.[15]

> (53) A: The cat will attack anyone won't
>   E: Oh yes <u>Well actually</u> she'll run for it <u>probably</u>
>   A: I suppose she's fully grown now
>   E: Fat
>   (S1A-019 162–166 FACE)

Actually signals an apology or concession in the face of some opposition or unexpected event. (The cat will not attack anyone but she'll probably run for it. I'm telling you this although you might not agree with me). (Cf. Beeching 2010: 153.) The reason for *actually* is politeness (avoiding making a face-threatening remark). *Actually* can also have a hedging effect when it occurs together with *sort of* and *kind of*:

> (54) A: Did you apply for anything in the final year
>   B: Apply for
>   A: Any jobs
>   B: I was actually I was actually quite keen
>   on getting out of education <,>
>   A: And uhm I was <u>actually kind of</u>
>   relishing <u>actually sort of</u> getting to June and
>   and just getting free and just thinking I'll get a job in a shop
>   (S1A-034 132–133 FACE)

3.11.4 Novelty and surprise

Actually can also be used to invoke counter-expectation. Speakers bring with them a number of beliefs and assumptions to the interaction. They can respond to both explicitly expressed claims and to claims which are contrary to their own expectations or a normative point-of-view (cf. Section 3.5.1.2). According to Traugott and Dasher (2002: 157), '"Adversativity" is . . . more often used for specific markers that SP/Ws [speakers/writers] use to signal that they are expressing beliefs or points of view contrary to their own or the interlocutors' expectations regarding the states of affairs under discussion'. When something is in conflict with normal expectations it can be judged to be remarkable or exceptional. Thus *actually* is closely associated with the '"novelty factor" that is so fundamental to most discourse' (2002: ibid.).

In (55) *actually* is used to prepare the hearer for something completely unexpected and contrary to what one would believe about Gerry (and therefore something that both speakers can laugh about).

(55) B: Just one
      A: OK <,,>
      You know Gerry <u>actually</u> talks refers to my
      mother's bedroom as the boudoir
      She doesn't <laugh>
      B: Seriously <,,>
      (S1A-023 011–015 FACE)

In (56) the speaker has just realised that he enjoyed the study of architecture. The speaker uses *actually* to highlight the information (treating it as surprising and unexpected):

(56) B: I kind of <,> I mean <,> I
      I started the course <,> thinking that uhm
      I'd sort of do the full seven
      years and stuff
      but like I'm just going through the
      course I just just realised that it was <u>actually</u>
      the st study of architecture I really enjoyed <,,>
      (S1A-034 014–016 FACE)

Actually can have inferences other than novelty and surprise. What is unexpected can also be undesirable as pointed out by Tognini-Bonelli (1993: 208), 'the semantic prosody prospected by *actually* is one of unexpectedness and often, unpleasantness.' In (57) the implication conveyed by *actually* is that something is undesirable:

(57) A: Wh what do you personally get out of
      <,> this particular dance <,>
      B: Uhm <,,> it <,,> I find that I
      have to <,> be more honest about the
      way that I work uhm <,>

in a lot of other contact-based dance work
you can <u>actually cheat</u> and not <,> give
your weight fully or uhm take weight fully
<,> and it becomes a bit <,> sort
of nothingy whereas with this you've really
got to <,> put your whole body <,>
into it and you can't sort of just
be thinking <,> sort of intellectually on the
side thinking
(S1A-002 129–132 FACE)

That you can actually cheat is regarded by the speaker as something undesirable in contrast with the type of dance work she is engaged in (I find that I have to be more honest doing my type of dancing). Surprise (and meanings such as unpleasantness) are typical of *actually* (and *really*) but not of *in fact* which expresses epistemic meaning and adversativity.

Actually can also occur in questions with the implication that an event is undesirable:

(58) B: Mm <,,> What's <u>actually</u> going to be happening on
uhm <,> Sunday
What are we going to do
is the idea that we just go for a walk around Richmond Park
A: Well Xepe seems to love this idea of having a picnic but I'm not too sure about this
B: Not if you've had lunch
A: Because I'll have eaten anyway
(S1A-006 024–030 FACE)

Actually implies that the speaker is not looking forward to the picnic. The idea of a picnic is regarded as problematic or undesirable since the speakers will already have eaten. On the other hand, when no component of surprise can be discovered *actually* (like *in fact*) is best classified as 'emphasising reality' (cf. the discussion by Lenk 1998: 155).

3.11.5 Emphasising the speaker's position

Another function which can be related to counter-expectation is illustrated by *actually* where it co-occurs with an expression of the speaker's opinion: *I think, I'll tell you, the thing is, I'm not sure, I mean*. The function of *actually* can be understood 'against the background assumption that some hearers might not agree with the proposition q, based on existing norms, beliefs and expectations in society' (Mortier and Degand 2009: 354). The adversative meaning is, however, only hinted at. In (59) the hedging or downtoning function is further indicated by *mm yeah mm mind you*.

(59) B: So it's actually a better quality chocolate
A: So there you go <,>
B: <u>Mm Yeah Mm Mind you</u> <u>actually I think</u> Tob's marvellous

Well I don't know <,,>
How did Peggy get on with her guitar
(S1A-023 174–181 FACE)

The adversative meaning of *actually* is not very strong in (59). In broadcast discussion, on the other hand, *actually I think* and *I think in fact* are used rhetorically to emphasise the speaker's position vis-à-vis other positions.

3.11.6 Elaboration

Tognini-Bonelli (1993) draws attention to the strategic uses of *actually* to take up a different position or 'changing the interpretative angle' by rephrasing or revising what has been said (rather than evoking opposition or counter-expectation). Along the same lines, Mortier and Degand (2009) distinguished six different functions of 'reformulation'. However, these were based on written rather than spoken material. In spoken language we can expect *actually* to have additional functions typical of conversation such as 'topic shift' and self-correction.

In (60) *actually* marks the change to a new perspective. The speaker has just explained why working in the dance group with disabled dancers is different from dancing with other groups and then changes the perspective to what is 'more true' or 'more important'.

(60) B: But working <,> in this group uhm <,,>
      it's <,> different in terms of uhm
      <,> the way <,> that you have to
      dance
      Actually you have to be much more honest
      about what you're doing <,> uhm
      (S1A-002 123–125 FACE)

When *actually* co-occurs with *I mean* it has been analysed as precision:

(61) A: OK so it's a limited number of
      museums
      B: Very limited
      I mean actually ethnographic museum work is very
      limited
      A: Right right <,>
      (S1A-066 065–067 FACE)

And actually occurred in 5 examples. *Actually* does more than elaborate on what has been said. In Clift's words (2001: 283), the *actually*-marked turn proposes 'something more noteworthy than what preceded it'.

(61) B: And I actually decided that because I'd
      always been sort of like told by teachers

ah you're good at this you should
do this and you should do this as
well because I was always really good at
science and stuff like that
<u>And actually</u> I'm more interested in in
in doing creative things than actually in science
(S1A-034 058–059 FACE)

Additional information can be given in the form of pointing out the consequences of what happened earlier (*so actually*) (causal).

(63) B: Uhm and so you know <,> the sort
of person for whom if you said I'm afraid that there's no you know
we're running out of tea bags or
something you know something's always going to
hitch
always something with her class <,>
<u>So actually</u> transporting them to another building could
be perceived to be a problem
(S1A-082 096–098 FACE)

3.11.6.1 Topic shift

Clift describes *actually* as a marker which introduces material which has a 'touched off character' linking back in some way to the preceding discourse without necessarily being an elaboration of what has been said (Clift 2001: 286). This function is illustrated in (64):

(64) C: Shall I call you at the weekend
and we'll do it early next week
<,> because uhm <,> I want to start
<,,>
<u>Actually</u> I'm going up to Barnet next
week to use my friend's computer for my course essay so <,> if I call
in with you one day on the way
up there or on the way back then
I've got the stuff
Cos I need it to revise
you need it to revise as well
(S1A-090 024–028 FACE)

The connection signalled by *actually* 'resides entirely in the discursive mind of the speaker (Mortier and Degand 2009: 357). *Actually* signals a 'mental leap' from one part of the discourse to another. This use is only weakly related to other elaborative uses of *actually* (ibid.).

3.11.6.2 'A change of mind'

Actually can also be 'a change of mind' marker. 'In such cases, the topical shift concerns a change of emphasis within a topic, with *actually* serving both to register the coming change of the topical direction and to signal the nature of the contribution as one that has just occurred to the speaker' Clift (2001: 281).

In (65), Speaker A signals by means of *oh actually* a change of mind and thus a shift in the direction of talk.

> (65) B: I can't bear it <,,>
>   Oh name please eat something <,,>
>   A: <u>Oh actually</u> Dad asked me if <,> Sarah
>   had phoned me on Sunday
>   I thought funny thing to ask <,>
>   And then I remembered of course she had
>   cos that was why we went over
>   (S1A-023 120–124 FACE)

Example (66) is similar. The combination *oh . . . actually* suggests that the speaker has suddenly remembered something, that is, *actually* signals a revision or change of mind:

> (66) A: No it was wonderful
>   We were travelling
>   <u>oh</u> we'd just left the Ashram <u>actually</u>
>   We were travelling with some <unclear-word> third class
>   very important people
>   (S1A-032 067–071 FACE)

3.11.6.3 Self-interruption and restart

A special kind of shift in the direction of talk is self-interruption followed by restart:

> (67) A: Well but they'll they'll probably you
>   know they'll probably hit a point where
>   <u>Actually</u> it's not necessarily such a bad
>   thing because the chances are that if they
>   leave it they'll never do it
>   (S1A-005 153–154 FACE)

The speaker interrupts herself (they'll hit a point where) and then starts again (actually it's not such a bad thing).

3.11.6.4 *Actually* as a softener in end position

Both *actually* and *in fact* have a softening or mitigating function in conversation especially at the end of the utterance. *Actually* is used to soften an opinion (signalled by *I think, I mean, I'm sure, I find, I don't know*). In the following example it also co-occurs with *well* and with pauses:

    (68) A: Does Does shouting a lot and making lots
          of noise really have much effect uh in
          terms of intercession or
          C: Well <,> I think it does actually
          Yeah I think I think equally you can do
          it quietly
          (S1A-068 196–200 FACE)

Actually I think forms a cluster in final position. The context also contains *mm* and *well*.

    (69) A: Yes
          Mm Well that all seems to go with him
          actually I think
          you think somehow
          Uhm <,,>
          (S1A-067 160–164 FACE)

Actually also occurs together with evaluative (degree) adjectives such as *good, nice, great* in the same utterance. It has a softening or hedging function coinciding with a weakening or disappearance of the adversative meaning.

    (70) D: I said you were <,> you know <,>
          tickled with it <,> thought it was great
          fun <,>
          B: Yup
          D: Very nice present actually <,>
          I mean she does work out good presents
          <,>
          (S1A-022 170–172 FACE)

The participants are referring to a present (a bag) which was intended as a joke because no one wanted to be seen around with it. *Actually* (pronounced with a rise-plus-fall tone) introduces an apologetic or defensive note in the face of possible objection.

    The speaker uses *actually* both as a softener and to sum up his comments on the singing performance he has just been listening to.

    (71) A: It's pretty It's nice A good chord actually <,>
          (S1A-026 263–266 FACE)

Actually in conversation can be overused and 'compulsive', that is, speakers cannot stop using it although it has no clear meaning.[16]

    (72) A: Well I'd actually like the same one
          back again actually
          If it's not too much trouble
          (S1A-080 112–114 FACE)

The examples have been analysed as hedging or softening.

3.12 Summarising *actually* in face-to-face conversation

Table 3.21 sums up the functions of *actually* in a sample of 200 examples from the ICE-GB.

Table 3.21 *Actually* in different functions in conversation

Adversative	
(Strong or weak) opposition (but actually, but . . . actually)	20
Emphasising reality	24
Novelty and surprise (counter-expectation)	46
Hedging and polite (mild contradiction)	21
Emphasising the speaker's position (I think actually)	16
Elaborative	
Clarification (I mean actually)	1
Upgrading	3
Elaboration (and actually)	2
Causal (so actually)	7
Conversation-specific	
Shifting the topic	9
Change of mind	5
Self-interruption and restart	2
Softener	44

Actually like *in fact* is an adversative marker. It has meanings such as strong or weak contradiction. However, it also has functions which can be directly related to the characteristics of informal conversation. *Actually* responds to features in the communication situation, for example, the need to downtone what is said in order to attend to the hearer's face needs. It is a characteristic feature of *actually* in informal conversation that it is used in end position as a softener. In addition, *actually* also has functions such as self-correction, change-of-mind and topic-shift which contribute to coherence in informal conversation.

The adversative and emphatic functions were more frequent than the elaborative function (see Table 3.22). This makes *actually* different from both *in fact* and the Dutch *eigenlijk* in Mortier and Degand's analysis.

Table 3.22 Distribution of *actually* in different core functions in conversations in the ICE-GB. Sample of 200 examples.

	ICE-GB		Mortier and Degand (%)
Adversative or emphatic (Mortier and Degand 'opposition')	127	63.5%	34.7%
Elaborative or softening (Mortier and Degand 'reformulation')	73	36.5%	29.2%
Total	200	100%	63.9%*

* Some examples were classified as 'no clear association'

3.13 *Actually* in public dialogue

Actually was less frequent in public dialogue than in face-to-face conversation and in telephone calls. See Table 3.23.

Table 3.23 The frequencies of *actually* in private and public dialogue.

	Frequency	Per 1,000,000	Number of words
Private dialogue	438	2,132	205,357
Public dialogue	290	1,695	171,062

We can make a comparison with *in fact* which was found more often in public dialogue. *Actually* was however more frequent in classroom lessons and in business transactions than in conversation.

3.13.1 *Actually* in classroom lessons

Actually was more frequent in classroom discourse than in other types of discourse. It was for instance almost five times as frequent as *in fact* in this discourse type . The frequencies of *actually* in different positions in the clause are shown in Table 3.24. *Actually* was found in medial position in 92 out of 98 examples; there were 4 examples in initial and 2 in final position.

Table 3.24 *Actually* in different positions in classroom lessons

Position	Number	Per cent	Comparison with face-to-face conversation
Initial	4	4.1%	21.5%
Medial	92	93.9%	56.5%
Final	2	2.0%	22%
Total	98	100%	100%

Actually was unusual together with pragmatic markers (although there were single examples of collocations with *so, and, sort of, uhm*).

A tutorial (classroom lesson) is more structured than an informal conversation and there are special speaker roles (tutor and student). Both the tutor and the students used *actually* (67 out of 98 examples were used by the tutor). The classroom interaction is characterised by question-answer exchanges. 9 questions with *actually* were asked by the tutor (A) and 2 by the student (C). The tutor's questions are of a special type and follow a classroom procedure. They are typically introduced by *and* and represent steps on the way to the conclusion of an argumentation. The tutor knows what answer he wants and comments on or elaborates on the answer he gets.

(73) A: It would be relaxed
That's exactly right

And <u>And what would it actually look like</u> <,>
Just what will the cells look like
Do you have any idea
...
A: Yes You were right they'd be changed but
they'd be atrophied
They would be actually smaller and and a
bit shrunken <unclear-words> Yes
C: <u>And what would actually happen with the</u> <,> <u>muscle tone</u>
(S1B–009 018–022 030–032 CLASSROOM LESSON)

The tutor's use of *actually* in questions (to which the answer is already known) is associated with the activity and with the speaker role. If *in fact* had been used instead this would have made the question conducive (a positive response would have been expected). The teacher could not have continued by saying 'do you have any idea?' as in the example above (Just what will the cells look like do you have any idea?).

Classroom discourse is characterised by the progression from one stage of the lesson to another. *Actually* is a contextualisation cue with the function of orienting the hearer as to what is taking place in the discourse. Example (74) is taken from a tutorial on religion. The law (the Hebrew bible) has been lagging behind the practice with regard to the restriction of worship to priests. The monopoly given to the priests has therefore been made into an institution. *(And . . . then) actually* was used by the tutor to shift the topic, to sum up the argumentation and to draw a conclusion.

(74) A: And in the time of P the reason
that the <,,> that the priests are given
this monopoly is that <,> they've got it
And uh Ezekiel can see it coming and
as he says in theory this is the
way it's got to be
<u>And it's then actually</u> made into an
institution It's
It's promulgated
It's decreed in the time after in
the time after Malachi
(S1B–001 114–118 CLASSROOM LESSON)

In (75) the context is causal. Cause –effect is signalled by *so* and the conditional construction. The tutor is demonstrating something to the students:

(75) A: What I wanted to do was
the painting like was <u>actually</u> affected by its
environment
<u>so if</u> it was hanging on an a
white gallery wall then that would <u>actually</u> affect
the painting
And if it was hanging on a piece

of wallpaper that would <u>actually</u> affect the picture
The picture is part of environment that it's <u>actually</u> in <,>
(S1B-018 012–016 CLASSROOM LESSON)

A has been taking photographs of a painting in order to study how it is affected by hanging on a white gallery wall or on a piece of wallpaper. *Actually* has little meaning in itself but gets its function from the interaction with the social situation. In addition to its contextual function (to indicate cause) it is an important marker of (the tutor's) authority and knowledgeability (cf. *in fact*).

Actually is used also when the tutor wants to demonstrate or explain something as a part of a longer argumentation:

(76) A: So between the Silurian and the Devonion is <,,> what <,>
      D: Bone beds
      C: Big <unclear words>
      A: There are the bonebeds but what happened <,>at the end of the Silurian<,>
      D: Large mountainbeds
      C: <unclear words>
      A: Exactly There's a mountain building up a major
      orogenic eve event <,>
      <u>Now if</u> we were <u>actually</u> looking at the
      stratigraphic column then we would <u>actually</u> s recognise
      there was a difference between the rocks that
      come before and the rocks that come afterwards
      in terms of their <,> age and appearance
      and character and so on and we would
      (S1B-006 142–144 CLASSROOM LESSON)

(76) illustrates how the teacher uses the sequence question-answer strategically to explain certain geological events relating to mountain building. After he has got the answer he wants (there's a mountain building up an orogenic event) he goes on to build up the argument (if we look at the stratigraphic column we would recognise the differences between the rocks). *Actually* serves an important argumentative purpose although the context does not involve opposition but cause.

In (77) the causal meaning is also signalled by 'that's why':

(77) A: That's exactly what happens in our eyes
      and <u>that's why</u> the nasal retina <u>actually</u>
      sees light <,> from the lateral field
      So what I see when I see my
      hand over here that is hitting my nasal
      retina over on this side over there
      (S1B-015 203–204 CLASSROOM LESSON)

Actually in the classroom was characterised by a mixture of features such as argumentative context, authority and knowledgeability associated with the teacher role, the use of exam questions and medial position. On the other hand, *actually* was not used to elaborate on a theme, for self-correction or to change the topic.

3.13.2 *Actually* in business transactions

Business transactions represent the text type where *actually* occurred with the highest frequency (also compared with *in fact*). It is therefore of interest to study how it is used. Just as in conversation *actually* is flexible. It is frequent both in initial and end position (see Table 3.25).

Table 3.25 *Actually* in different positions in business transactions

Position	Number	Per cent	Comparison with face-to-face conversation
Initially	9	16%	21.5%
Medially	35	60%	56.5%
End	14	24%	22%
Total	58	100%	100%

Actually co-occurred with *sort of* (2 examples), *because, so, oh think*. It was found after a pause (2 examples) and with a following pause (1 example). Similarly to conversation there were examples of clusters of pragmatic markers (*I mean well actually, uh<,>, actually I think*).

In a business transaction the participants typically try to come to a consensus by negotiation. For example, the participants have to come to a decision about how to rebuild their shower room (where to place the door, where the soap tray goes, etc.). In (78) *actually* is used by the speaker to argue her point in the guise of elaboration. 'The best place for the soap tray is not at the end (of the bathtub) but under the shower'.

> (78) A: Yeah or or or d or d or down at one end probably best you know so it's not not filling up with water at o one <u>Actually</u> the ideal place for a soap tray is under the shower so it doesn't fill up with water
> (S1B-071 190–191 BUSINESS TRANSACTION)

In (79), the participants are negotiating how much money they can afford to spend on the children's clothing. According to speaker A, if you were to keep the receipts it would add up and you would think that was more than you had thought:

> (79) A: Uhm yes yes yes it is
> Uhm <,> and
> <u>and I think actually</u> it's quite telling
> because if you were to do that and
> add it up at the end of the
> six months you think
> oh you know I had to <,,>
> that was more than I thought

I had to <,> rekit for all sorts of things
(S1B-072 130–136 BUSINESS TRANSACTION)

In example (80) from the same business transaction, the speaker emphasises her opinion that children are a big item of expenditure thus distinguishing herself from the 'normative' viewpoint that the maintenance of children is not a great expense. In the business transaction *I think actually* is used as a strategy to achieve a goal. *Actually* has the specialised function of 'emphasising the individual position of the speaker in opposition to other possible positions' (cf. Biber and Finegan 1988: 26). We can make a comparison with face-to-face conversation where *I think actually* is used to hedge the speaker's opinion (Section 3.11.5).

(80) A: Because <u>I think</u> that's <u>actually</u> usually and especially with children of the ages
they are <,> a pretty big item of expenditure
and I think inevitably people say oh
(S1B-072 141–143 BUSINESS TRANSACTION)

Actually co-occurs with *I mean* rather than *I think:*

(81) A: Well it's it's not it's
not so crucial up here
<u>I mean well actually</u> it is
<u>I mean</u> where there's a sort of
upper storey <,> it's all a bit
higgledy-piggledy I mean you know
(S1B-073 107–109 BUSINESS TRANSACTION)

In final position, on the other hand, *actually* is softening. The speaker does not say 'that's not right' but uses different strategies such as *I'm not quite sure* and *actually* to downtone the assertion:

(82) A: Uh the History of Art department has one
uh member of staff who's on an
academically-related scale
uh the Map Librarian in Geography is on
an academically-related scale and <,> there are three
in English I think
<u>I'm not quite sure if that's</u>
<u>right actually</u>
(S1B-075 021–023 BUSINESS TRANSACTION)

To summarise, in a business negotiation the goal is to come to an agreement by negotiation rather than by argumentation. *Actually* has the function of negotiating claims, for instance, by emphasising the speaker's position vis-à-vis what other people may think. *Actually* co-occurs with *I think* and is closely associated with counter-expectation (taking up a stance towards other positions or expectations). *Actually* was also used to soften a claim made by the speakers in the transaction (especially in final position).

3.14 *Actually* in monologues

Actually was twice as frequent in dialogue as in monologue. In unscripted monologues it was most frequent in demonstrations.

3.14.1 *Actually* in demonstrations

In demonstrations both *actually* and *in fact* are frequent and can be used with similar functions. In demonstrations *actually* occurred even more often than in face-to-face or telephone conversations (and it is also more frequent than *in fact*). However, *actually* (unlike *in fact*) occurred almost only in medial position (1 example in initial position; 1 example in final position). Moreover, *actually* and *in fact* can have different meanings if the context involves opposition. *Actually* is used with a polite and hedging function as in the following example which comes from a biology lecture:

> (83) It's not in the red blood cells. It's <u>actually</u> cells of our body. And <,>very luckily for us their enzyme spectrum has an absorption spectrum that changes depending on whether the enzyme is oxygenated or deoxygenated
> (S2A-053 025 DEMONSTRATION)

In fact would be strengthening and upgrading if the context is oppositive (It is not in the red blood cells – it is in cells of our body).

On the other hand, *actually* and *in fact* are both used to introduce explanations and clarifications and they can occur together in the same text as in the following example. *And actually* conveys that something is new and remarkable. Both *actually* and *in fact* convey some adversative meaning associated with a conflict with expectations and beliefs held by members of the research community.

> (84) This fits into the category of cells that <u>actually</u> glide. As you can see it fits into the motorised sausage concept. But we have no real idea how that's achieved except to say that it does move and it does require a substrate. And uh in general you can tell whether these require substrates or not because they stay in focus. If you get something swimming in the substrate then it won't <,,> Since they contain chlorophyll you can <u>in fact</u> change your optics to fluorescence. <u>And actually</u> the chloroplast shines up in that way
> (S2A-051 077–083 DEMONSTRATION)

To summarise, in demonstrations *actually* and *in fact* are used with different meanings if the context involves opposition. *In fact* has a strengthening or upgrading function while *actually* is mildly contradictory and is used to hedge correction (as in face-to-face conversation). However, both *in fact* and *actually* were more typically used for explanation in causal rather than adversative contexts in demonstrations (*Since they contain chlorophyll . . . you can in fact / actually . . .*). *Actually* can also be indexed to authority and a particular speaker role (lecturer). In the causal meaning *actually* highlights the novelty and remarkable quality of the results.

3.15 *Actually* in writing

Actually in writing was frequent in social letters. It was also frequent in academic and non-academic writing especially in the humanities and social sciences. Another category where it was frequent was student examination scripts. In social letters it is used in the same way as in conversation to establish or maintain harmonious relations.

(85)   Yesterday we went up another mountain on the
        tram - Mount Tibidales
        It was gorgeous up there because it was
        so cold in fact in fact by the time
        I came home I was <u>actually</u> freezing cold
        and goose pimply
        (W1B-009 042–043 SOCIAL LETTERS)

3.16 Summarising *actually*

Summing up, we have seen that *actually* is used in different ways depending on the context where it is used. The context includes not only the linguistic context but the occurrence in speech or writing, monologue or dialogue, the text type and the situation. It was most frequent in conversation where *actually* was used to strengthen co-operation and to establish familiarity and solidarity by conveying an apology or a defensive attitude with regard to some opposition. In writing *actually* was used in social letters. This can be expected since the writer wants to be informal and establish intimacy with the recipient.

When *actually* was used in other text types (such as classroom discourse or business transactions) it had specialised functions (including 'strategic uses' and indexical stance meanings). An example is the function 'emphasis of personal position' which was frequent in business transactions where speakers express their opinions in order to persuade another speaker and come to a decision. In the classroom *actually* was frequently used by the teacher or the tutor in explanations or demonstrations which are part of an ongoing argumentation with a particular goal. In demonstrations *actually* had the additional function of emphasising the novelty of a result or the speaker's role as an authority.

3.17 Comparing *in fact* and *actually*

The research question in this work is how pragmatic markers are affected by the text type (activity type or social situation). The focus has been on *in fact* and *actually*. They have a similar meaning and they are often treated together. However, we know very little about how they vary across text types and situations, speech and writing, monologue and dialogue. Table 3.26 shows how *in fact* and *actually* vary formally and functionally with regard to different parameters.

Table 3.26 *In fact* and *actually* compared

	In fact	*Actually*
Regional variation	No difference between British and American English	Mainly British English
Style	Formal	Informal
Speech or writing	More characteristic of speech than writing	More characteristic of speech than writing
Monologue or dialogue	Mainly monological	Mainly dialogical
Text type	Typically (frequently) occurring in legal cross-examination, demonstration, broadcast discussion; in writing it typically occurs in business letters	Typically (frequently) occurring in classroom lessons, telephone calls, face-to-face conversation, demonstration, business transaction; in writing it typically occurs in social letters
Changes over time	Becoming less frequent	Becoming more popular
Position (face-to-face conversation)	**initial *end medial	**medial position end initial
Prosody	Both stressed and unstressed Occurs with pauses	Both stressed and unstressed Does not occur with pauses
Typical collocations	*but*	*well, and, actually, but*
Primary function	Adversative Elaboration Counter-expectation Factuality	Adversative Elaboration Counter-expectation Factuality
Adversative or elaborative	Primarily elaborative	Primarily adversative
Typical sub-senses	Expressing explicit or implicit opposition, upgrading	Mild contradiction, hedging, topic shift, punctuation
Specialised meanings (examples)	The use in cross-examinations by the examiner to ask questions to which both the speaker and the hearer know the answer	The use in classroom lessons by the tutor to present explanations in a particular order
Indexical factors (examples)	Speaker role (examiner, lecturer)	Speaker role (teacher, lecturer)

* Frequent ** Very frequent

There is not a categorical difference between *in fact* and *actually*. They occur for example in the same text types but with different frequencies. *In fact* was used in text types which are formal (it was more frequent in public dialogue than in private dialogue). It was most frequent in business letters in the written text types. It was typically used in argumentative contexts such as court examination and broadcast discussion. Both *in fact* and *actually* could have 'specialised' meanings depending on text type. In cross-examinations the 'factual' meaning of *in fact* was exploited by the speaker (the cross-examiner) to ask a question the answer to which is already known to the participants in order to show the events in a certain light. *Actually*, on the other hand, was above all frequent in conversation where it had functions such as hedging and politeness. It was also used redundantly and 'compulsively' with a mainly interpersonal function.

Position is probably the most important formal feature constraining the interpretation of *in fact* and *actually*. For example, the large number of *in fact* in initial position indicates that it has an important role to create coherence by elaborating on a preceding conversational turn and to show the speaker's involvement with the hearer and the topic. An interesting observation was that *in fact* and *actually* have different positions depending on the text type (and whether they occur in speech or in writing). The frequency of *in fact* and *actually* in medial position in demonstrations co-occurs with other functions such as explaining something to a public.

Moreover, the importance of speaker role is reflected in the frequencies with which *in fact* and *actually* is used by different speakers. For example, *in fact* was frequently used by the 'examiner' and less frequently by the plaintiff in courtroom examinations. In the classroom *actually* was used by the tutor or lecturer rather than by the student. Less directly a pragmatic marker can index features such as authority and power.

Notes

1. The use of *in fact* as VP adverbial (in practice, as far as can be told from evidence, in actuality) will not be discussed here. (Cf. Schwenter and Traugott 2000: 11.
2. Statistical significance has been computed using the Log Likelihood Calculator.
3. The DCPSE was compiled in order to make it possible to study short-term changes in spoken English. It consists of a comparable number of texts from the ICE-GB and the LLC representing different categories such as face-to-face conversation, telephone conversation, broadcast discussion, broadcast interviews, spontaneous commentary, parliamentary language, legal cross-examination, assorted spontaneous and prepared speech. The examples from the ICE Corpus are collected from a sub-corpus of 421,362 words and the examples from the LLC Corpus from a corresponding sub-corpus of 464,074 words.
4. We can make a comparison with the whole LLC Corpus where 40 examples were completely unstressed (95 examples had the onset and 74 examples had weak stress). 130 examples had the nuclear tone.
5. In the London-Lund Corpus, 9 out of 19 examples in initial position were also separated from the rest of the sentence by a tone unit boundary.
6. A third meaning is represented *in fact₁* (a VP adverbial) with the literal meaning 'in fact' (not in theory
7. The pronunciation of *in fact* in example (4) was not possible to determine.
8. Moreover *so . . . in fact* (with intervening words between *so* and *in fact*) was found in 3 examples and *and . . . in fact* in 1 example.
9. Speaker C and D in the cross-examinations are interrogated as witnesses. Speaker C used 10 examples of *in fact* and speaker D 3 examples.
10. One example was difficult to classify.
11. Mortier and Degand discuss French *en fait* and Dutch *eigenlijk* (actually).
12. Taglicht (2001) distinguishes between *actually₂* (initial, parenthetical and final) and *actually₁*. (integrated in the sentence structure). No distinction has been made here between different uses of *actually* in medial position.

13. All the examples (392 examples) from face-to-face conversation have been included.
14. This is similar to Mortier and Degand's use of the term 'adversative' also discussed in Section 3.5.1.2: '[w]e will refer to *en fait* and its equivalents as "adversatives"; with the understanding that their semantics provides for more subtle values than a strict oppositive one' (Mortier and Degand 2009: 342).
15. As suggested in Section 3.5.3 this function was also found with *in fact*, in particular when it co-occurred with hesitation markers. It was, however, less typical of *in fact*. Similarly, Mortier and Degand (2009: 356) found that *eigenlijk* was found more often with attenuation function than *en fait* but the difference was not large.
16. In French, on the other hand, this 'compulsive' usage is typical of *en fait* (Simon-Vandenbergen and Willems 2011).

4

General Extenders

4.1 Introduction

The following example illustrates the use of general extenders:

> and strangely enough my qualifications look quite relevant because of their titles
> <u>and things</u> <,> you know about dress and perfume <u>and stuff like that</u> (ICE–GB)

And things and *and stuff like that* are placed at the end of the utterance or a phrase and extend the utterance by referring to a category 'in the air'.[1] The study of general extenders has mostly focused on a single variety. This variety is usually British English as the example above. However, we also need studies comparing general extenders in different languages and varieties of English. According to Evison et al. (2007: 156), 'Models based on high-attention languages such as English tend to dominate; research examining other languages in their own right can serve to ratify or challenge English-dominant models. The same applies to varieties within languages such as English where certain varieties have dominated.'

General extenders can be considered a global phenomenon which can be studied across different languages. Terraschke and Holmes (2007) compared general extenders in New Zealand English and German and Norrby and Winter (2002) highlighted Swedish and Australian adolescents' use of general extenders for purposes of affiliation.

The regional angle, in particular at the national level, has long been neglected in variational studies (Schneider and Barron 2008; Barron and Schneider 2009). The aim of the present study is to contribute to the still small number of quantitative studies of variation in the use of discourse features by comparing the forms and functions of general extenders in several national varieties of English. Speakers of different varieties of English use general extenders differently which opens up the possibility that the choice of a particular general extender reflects social norms and can create a certain regional or national identity.

The study of geographical variation has been impeded by the lack of comparable data from different languages or language varieties. The situation has now changed and we use comparable corpora for a quantitative and qualitative study of similarities and differences between several national varieties of English. Another aim is therefore to investigate how regional corpora can be used to compare national varieties.

The structure of this chapter is as follows. Section 4.2 reviews previous work. In Section 4.3 I describe the structural variability of general extenders and their potential creativity. Section 4.4 discusses the selection of corpora. Section 4.5 gives some quantitative information about *and* and *or* extenders in some national varieties of English. Section 4.6 discusses the factors involved in explaining regional varieties. Section 4.7 contains the concluding discussion.

4.2 Previous work

General extenders have been studied from many different aspects. This is not surprising since they are realised in a variety of ways. Their formal variation has encouraged sociolinguistic variationist approaches to general extenders. In a pioneering work, Dines (1980) suggested that 'the set-marking tag'[2] *and all that* could be studied as a sociolinguistic discourse variable ('a socially diagnostic feature') in the Labovian tradition of variational sociolinguistics.

According to Dines (1980: 16), the heuristic procedure for isolating a discourse variable begins with the salience of some variant for some member of the speech community, proceeds to an analysis of its distribution, then to the postulation of an underlying form and the final mapping of the alternative variants. On the basis of this procedure Dines was able to show that the variation exhibited by the 'set-marking tag' was closely associated with the socio-economic class of the speakers. Dines described a common 'set-marking' function for the extenders. The tags introduced by *and* or by *or* could be identified as having the function 'to cue the listener to interpret the preceding element as an illustrative example of some more general case' (1980: 22). One of Dines's examples is:

> B: "Does your husband drink much?"
> A: "Not much. He'll have a drink at a party an' that"

The addition of the tag *and that* 'cues the listener to extract not only the specific meaning of "*party*" but the more general meanings of "he's a social drinker" or "he drinks occasionally' (Dines 1980: 22).

Dines's analysis of the extender as illustrative of a more general set recurs in other descriptions of the general extender. However, in more recent work the focus has changed to the functions that general extenders have in the interaction and in particular their affective or interpersonal functions.

In the last decade the investigation of the social functions of general extenders has exploded. The forms and uses of general extenders have been studied in relation to factors such as social class, age and gender. Pichler and Levey noticed dramatic changes in the frequencies of individual general extenders in a northern English dialect supporting earlier observations 'that scholars need to look beyond the linguistic conditioning to the social embedding of language in order to fully understand the renewal of individual variants' (Pichler and Levey 2011: 464). Cheshire (2007: 188) noted, for example, a working-class preference for *and that* and a middle-class preference for *and stuff* and *and things* in her material. She also found evidence for a possible north–south divide with *and things* used less often in the north. In the data analysed here there is a divide between British English (*and things* is more frequent than *and stuff* or other variants such as *and that* or *and all that*).

There is also a concentration of adolescent speakers using certain extenders such as *and stuff*. Winter and Norrby (2000: 6) argue that general extenders are used 'for the construction and performance of youth identities' (cf. Tagliamonte and Denis 2010: 344). Stenström et al. (2002) have shown on the basis of the Bergen Corpus of London Teenage Language (COLT) that adolescents used different types of general extenders to adults and that they used them more frequently. Of special interest is Tagliamonte and Denis's (2010) study of general extenders in the English spoken by adolescents in Canada. The authors observe that 'discourse-pragmatic features may differ markedly across varieties' (2010: 335), an observation which is corroborated in this work. However in Tagliamonte and Denis's study the focus is on social and linguistic rather than regional influences on discourse-pragmatic variation.

In 'contemporary' studies of general extenders the focus is also on their interaction with extra-linguistic contextual features. They are resources exploited by speakers in the communication situation in interaction with contextual features to express a number of different functions. They can be used to avoid saying too much; they can express attitudes and feelings and they can be used indexically to establish a social persona or a regional identity.

O'Keeffe has studied vague category markers (including general extenders) in an Irish radio phone-in show and shown that they indexed the participants as 'a socially aware middle-class group' with an interest in (Irish) social practices (O'Keeffe 2004: 15). General extenders are also associated with text type. Some research by McCarthy and O'Keeffe (2002) compares general extenders in national phone-in shows with conversational data in a large corpus. Preliminary results showed that certain forms were not as frequent as in casual conversations among friends and that speakers referred to different types of social knowledge depending on the text type. Cheng (2007) examined general extenders (and other uses of vague language) across representative samples of academic, business, conversational and public sub-corpora of Hong Kong English and compared the results with similar data from native speaker corpora. She showed for example that native English speakers used *or something* more often speakers of Hong Kong English. A possible explanation for this difference 'that requires further study' is that speakers of Hong Kong English are more formal in their language use than native speakers (Cheng 2007: 176).

4.3 Formal structure of general extenders

Initially, general extenders are best described with regard to their structure rather than on the basis of a common function. A 'formal' approach allows us to collect a large number of general extenders which can be further analysed with regard to their functional and contextual variability.

General extenders can be realised in many different ways. In order to describe their fixedness, variability and potential creativity we can postulate a restricted number of collocational frames from which different patterns can be derived by operations (construction rules; Terraschke 2007: 148) such as shortening or lexical replacement (e.g. substituting *thing* for *stuff*). The collocational frames contain *and* and *or* followed by a generic noun or an indefinite pronoun. In addition to the long forms such as *and things (stuff) like that* there are short, routinised forms such as *and things* or *and stuff*. *And that* can be constructed from *and that sort/kind of thing/stuff*. *And all* and *and all that* can be related to *and all that sort of thing*. *Or something* and *or anything* are abbreviated 'or-forms'. The connective can be missing (*o things like that*). Moreover, we find invariable, completely fixed forms such as *or so, or what, or whatever, and so on*.

Some examples of collocational frames and the extenders which can be constructed from them are shown below.[3] *Thing* may for instance be replaced by *stuff*. There is a choice between a short and a long form. Elements can be added (*and those stupid things*) by using the flexibility of the collocation frames.

Connective	Pre-modifier	Generic noun	Comparative	Demonstrative
And	kind of/sort of stupid	things/stuff (rubbish, shit)[4]	like	that/this

Without connective: things like that/this, stuff like that/this
Short forms: and things, and stuff
Long forms: and things like that/this, and stuff like that/this

Connective	Demonstrative	Comparative	Generic
And	that/this	kind/sort of	thing/stuff

Without connective: that/this kind of thing, that/this kind of stuff
Short form: and that

Connective	Quantifier	Comparative	Demonstrative
Or	something/anything	like	that/this

Without connective: something like that, anything like that
Short forms: or something, or anything

Connective	Quantifier (+ generic noun)	Comparative	Demonstrative
And	all things/everything	like	that/this

Connective	Quantifier + demonstrative	Comparative	Generic
And	all that/this	kind/sort of	thing/stuff
And	all those/these	kind(s)/sort of	things[5]
And	all that	(other)	stuff
And	all these	(different)	things

The 'and all' extender is productive in all varieties. The Santa Barbara Corpus contained the following variants: *and all this stuff, and all kinds of stuff, and all this shit, and all that other stuff, and all this bullshit, and all that shit, and all these different things, and all this other shit, and all this other stuff, and all this kind of thing, and all that stuff.*

4.4 Data

Variational pragmatics is by its nature comparative, that is, there must be at least two varieties that are compared with each other. Barron and Schneider (2009: 429) formulate a 'contrastivity principle' which is essential in all variational research: 'Linguistic features can be considered variety-specific only if the variety under study is contrasted with at least one other variety of the same kind and of the same language'. Pragmatic features in British English can, for instance, be contrasted with similar features in American English or Canadian English.

Comparative cross-variety studies have to start somewhere and we are now lucky to be able to use the national components of ICE (the International Corpus of English) for systematic comparisons across several varieties of English. The ICE corpora are especially tailored for studies ranging over national varieties and will make it possible to make confident statements about 'World Englishes' rather than a single variety. According to Mair (2009: 10), '[s]uch cross-variety comparative research is much needed in studies on World Englishes and was one of the foremost goals envisaged by the founders of the ICE-project'.

The ICE-project (the International Corpus of English project) was initiated in order to enable comparisons across regional varieties of English including some second-language varieties: 'A major feature of the ICE philosophy is that it embraces ESL countries systematically in addition to ENL countries' (Schmied 1996: 182). The ICE corpora can be regarded as comparable since they were compiled according to the same principles. The texts in the corpus 'generally date from 1990 to 1999 inclusive' (Nelson 1996: 28). Each corpus consists of written English (600,000 words) and spoken English (400,000 words).[6] General extenders occur above all in spoken English and with the highest frequency in 'informal spoken conversation among familiars' (Overstreet 1999: 6). The searches I have carried out were therefore restricted to dialogue (private and telephone conversation) in the corpora examined. The corpora used are the British component of the ICE Corpus (ICE-GB), the Australian component (ICE-AUS), the New Zealand Corpus (ICE-NZ), the Canadian ICE-Corpus (ICE-CAN) and the Singapore ICE corpus (ICE-SIN). An American ICE-Corpus is still lacking. However, the Santa Barbara Corpus of Spoken American English (SBC) provides the source of date for the spontaneous spoken part of the International Corpus of English (http://www.linguistics.ucsb.edu/research/sbcorpus.html [accessed 4 October 2012]). The corpus is larger than the spontaneous parts of the sub-corpora I have used from the other varieties (249,000 words of spoken English). The frequencies of extenders in the corpora compared have therefore been normalised to 1,000,000 words.

The conversations recorded are generally produced by educated speakers (and are therefore not a demographically representative cross-section of the population) (cf. Mair 2009: 9). It follows that some speakers may have been excluded.[7] In the American corpus there are, for example, no speakers of Black English although a number of regional dialects are represented.[8]

The sub-corpora were selected in order to make it possible to compare general extenders across regional varieties of different kinds. British, American, Canadian, New Zealand and Australian English representative of the 'Englishes' belonging to Kachru's Inner Circle. English is acquired as a first language and is not learnt in an institutionalised educational context.

ICE–SIN, on the other hand, represents an outer circle variety of one of the New Englishes (Platt, Weber and Ho 1984). The language situation in Singapore has been described as unique with English co-occurring with local languages. English is 'the First Language' and children are also educated in his/her native language. Speakers of Singaporean English may therefore use general extenders in the same way as speakers of English as a foreign language rather than as native speakers. On the informal level we find a local variant Singlish (Colloquial Singaporean English) being used. Regional varieties are distinguished (or similar) with respect to conversational style, social or cultural values associated with appropriateness or politeness. These norms may also differ within a society. In the developmental scenario suggested by Schneider (2007), Singaporean English has reached a stage characterised by a high degree of cultural and linguistic independence and the acceptance of an indigenous linguistic identity.

According to Schneider, 'Singaporean English has come to be the means of expression of this newly emerging Asian-cum-western culture' (Schneider 2007: 156). In such varieties a general extender may have a social value associated with Asian rather than Western culture. Singaporean English has for instance been described as a dialect 'to express emotionality and proximity or to play with' (Schneider 2007: 158).

The ICE Corpora include other varieties where the speech situation can be described as multilingual. New Zealand English has been described as being of the 'the British "type"' (Columbus 1999: 402). However native speakers of Maori use a different conversational style from non-Maori or Pakeha speakers when they speak English (Holmes 1996). As Stubbe and Holmes (2000) point out, 'Maori conversational style is typically more strongly based on shared knowledge than that typical of Pakeha speakers'. Another observation they make (quoting Britain 1992: 95) is that 'conversational solidarity is a particularly important goal for speakers in Pacific societies and is expressed in a number of ways that linguists class as markers of "positive politeness."'

Searches in the corpora were made on the basis of combinations such as *and things like that* as well as shorter forms such *and things, things like that, or something*, etc. and single words such as *stuff* and *thing* in order to capture all the possibilities. Examples where there was a break in the extender because of laughter or hesitation were included where I noticed them. It is, however, possible that some variants may have been missed especially if they are unusual.[9]

4.5 Distribution of general extenders across varieties

An advantage of the ICE-corpora is that we can compare the distribution of the frequencies of general extenders across varieties. A quantitative analysis is particularly useful when a certain extender competes with other variants, for example when there is variation between *things* and *stuff*.

The differences in frequency between regional varieties are remarkable. The highest number of extenders (both *and* or *or* extenders) was found in the ICE-AUS (2,440 examples) followed by ICE-SIN (2,250 examples) as shown in Table 4.1 and Figure 4.1. In order to achieve maximal comparability between the corpora normalised frequencies have been used (cf. Pichler 2010: 594).

Table 4.1 Total number of extenders in different varieties. The frequencies have been normalised to 1,000,000 words.

	ICE-GB		SBC		ICE-AUS		ICE-CAN		ICE-NZ		ICE-SIN	
And-extenders	T	Norm.	T	Norm.	T	Norm.	T	Norm.	T	Norm.	T	Norm.
Sub-total	129	645	191	765	189	945	28	140	254	1,270	221	1,105
Or-extenders												
Sub-total	133	665	220	883	289	1,445	43	215	123	615	191	955
Total	262	1,310	411	1,648	478	2,390	71	355	377	1,885	412	2,060

Norm. = Normalised frequencies (1,000,000 words) T = Token

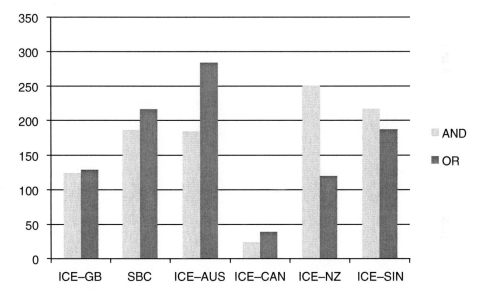

Figure 4.1 *And*- and *or*- extenders across varieties

There were more disjunctive *or*-extenders (including the zero-variants) than *and*-extenders (including the zero-variants) in SBC and ICE-AUS; the number of *or*-extenders was particularly high in Australian English. (In the SBC the difference was not statistically significant.) In ICE-NZ and ICE-SIN, on the other hand, *and*-extenders were predominant; These differences are statistically significant. In the ICE-GB, as well as in ICE–CAN, *and*-extenders and *or*-extenders were found in similar proportions[10] (see Table 4.2).

Table 4.2 *And-* and *or-* extenders compared in the corpora

	ICE-GB		SBC		ICE-AUS		ICE-CAN		ICE-NZ		ICE-SIN	
	n.	%	n.	%	n.	%	n.	%	n.	%	n.	%
And- extenders	129	49.2%	191	46.4%	189	39.5%	28	39.4%	254	67.4%	221	53.6%
Or- extenders	133	50.8%	220	53.5%	289	60.5%	43	60.6%	123	32.6%	191	46.4%
Total	262	100%	411	100%	478	100%	71	100%	377	100%	412	100%
		n.s.		n.s.		p<.001		p<.05		p<.001		p<.05

n. = number n.s. = not significant

The examples can be grouped according to whether they begin with *and* or with *or*. There is a large number of patterns with *and* (Table 4.3).

There were more than twice as many *and*-extenders in New Zealand English as in British English. The number of variants, is lowest in ICE-CAN. In the ICE-CAN there was, for example, no example of *and things* (31 examples in ICE-GB) or *and all that* (11 examples in ICE-AUS, 120 examples in ICE-SIN).

The difference between variants using *stuff* and *things* is striking. See Table 4.4.

Table 4.4 Forms with *stuff* and with *thing* in different varieties

	ICE-GB		SBC		ICE-AUS		ICE-CAN		ICE-NZ		ICE-SIN	
	T	Norm.	T	Norm.	T	Norm.	T	Norm.	T	Norm.	T	Norm.
Stuff	32	160	107	429	77	385	7	35	105	525	10	50
Thing	48	240	11	40	20	100	8	40	29	145	29	145
		n.s.		p<.001		p<.001		n.s.		p<.001		p<.01

Norm. = Normalised frequencies (1,000,000 words) n.s. = not significant T = Token

And stuff has been said to be generally more widespread in North American varieties than in other varieties (Overstreet and Yule 1997, Tagliamonte and Denis 2007, Pichler and Levey 2011). Tagliamonte and Denis (2007: 362) describe the use of *and stuff* (replacing *and things*) in their Toronto data as a 'dramatic' ongoing change 'encroaching on the adjunctive GE [general extender] system in the twentieth century'. The change is not evidenced in ICE-CAN but *stuff* is spreading fast to other varieties (such as Australian and New Zealand English) as shown from data representing different varieties of English.

In the ICE-data a form with *stuff* dominated in ICE-NZ, SBC, and ICE-AUS[12] while *things* was more frequent in British English and in Singapore English. In ICE-CAN, *thing* and *stuff* were equally frequent.

Table 4.5 compares short and long *and*-extenders with *stuff* and with *thing*.

Table 4.3 *And*-extenders in ICE-GB, SBC, ICE-AUS, ICE-CAN, ICE-NZ and ICE-SIN

	ICE-GB		SBC		ICE-AUS		ICE-CAN		ICE-NZ		ICE-SIN	
	T	Norm.	T	Norm.	T	Norm.	T	Norm.	T	Norm.	T	Norm.
Forms with *stuff*												
And stuff	19	95	70	281	53	265	2	10	85	425	4	20
And stuff like that	13	65	14	56	16	80	4	20	7	35	6	30
Other long *stuff* forms	–	–	23*	92	8**	40	1	5	13***	65	–	–
Forms with *things*												
(And) things	31	155	3	12	9	45	–	–	26	130	1	5
(And) things like that	12	60	4	16	11	55	4	20	17	85	22	110
Other long *thing* forms	5	25	4	16	–	–	4	20	12	60	7	35
Forms with other nouns[11]	6	30	11	44	2	10	–	–	5	25	3	15
Forms with *all*												
And everything	17	85	40	160	42	210	2	10	19	95	17	85
And everything like that	1	5	–	–	–	–	–	–	1	5	–	–
And everything else	–	–	–	–	–	–	–	–	2	10	3	15
And all that/this	5	25	8	32	11	55	1	5	10	50	120	600
And all	2	10	6	24	3	15	–	–	2	10	19	95
Other *and*-extenders												
And so on (and so forth)	17	85	8	32	12	60	10	50	7	35	19	95
And that	1	5	–	–	22	110	–	–	48	240	–	–
Total	129	645	191	765	189	945	28	140	254	1,270	221	1,105

Norm = Normalised frequencies (1,000,000 words) T = Token

* SBC: *and all that stuff* (7), *and all kinds of stuff*, *and all that sort of stuff*, *and all this other stuff* (3), *stuff like that*, *all kinds of stuff*, *all that stuff*, *and all this stuff* (2), *and all of that other stuff*, *and all kinds of stuff*, *and all stuff and junk* (2), *and that kinda stuff*, *and all that sorta stuff*

** ICE-AUS: *and all that kind of stuff*, *and all this sort of stuff* (2), *and all of this stuff*, *and all that stuff*, *and all that kind of stuff*, *and all that stuff of any sort*, *and that sort of stuff*

*** ICE-NZ: *and all that sort of stuff* (8), *and all that kind of stuff* (2), *all that stuff*, *and this stuff*, *this sort of stuff*

Table 4.5 Short and long forms of the *and*-extenders in ICE-GB, SBC, ICE-AUS, ICE-CAN, ICE-NZ and ICE-SIN[13]

	ICE-GB		SBC		ICE-AUS		ICE-CAN		ICE-NZ		ICE-SIN	
	T.	Norm.	T.	Norm.	T.	Norm.	T.	Norm.	T.	Norm.	T.	Norm.
Forms with *stuff*												
And stuff	19	95	70	281	53	265	2	10	85	425	4	20
Long forms with *stuff*	13	65	37	148	24	120	5	35	20	100	6	30
Forms with *things*												
And things	31	155	3	12	9	45	–	–	26	130	1	5
Long forms with *things*	48	240	8	32	11	55	8	40	29	145	29	145

Norm. = Normalised frequencies (1,000,000 words) T = token

And stuff was more frequent than a long form in ICE-GB, SBC, ICE-AUS and ICE-NZ. In Canadian English *and things* did not occur but only *and things like that* (and other long varieties). *And things like that* (and other long varieties) was also the most frequent *and*-extender in Singapore English. (In ICE- SIN and ICE-CAN the long forms dominated.) When we look at forms with *thing* the short form was more frequent only in ICE-GB and in ICE-NZ.

In comparison with *and* there are few patterns with *or* (7 in all).[14] *Or* is followed by a form with *something* (*anything*) or a *wh*-form (*or whatever, or what*) (Table 4.6).

Table 4.6 *Or*-extenders in ICE-GB, SBC, ICE-AUS, ICE-CAN, ICE-NZ and ICE-SIN

	ICE-GB		SBC		ICE-AUS		ICE-CAN		ICE-NZ		ICE-SIN	
	T	Norm.	T	Norm.	T	Norm.	T	Norm.	T	Norm.	T	Norm.
Or something	61	305	124	498	185	925	9	45	50	250	63	315
Or something like that/this (and other long variants)	7	35	14	56	29	145	6	30	16	80	43	215
Or anything	23	115	27	108	30	150	1	5	24	120	13	65
Or anything like that	7	35	1	4	5	25	3	15	5	25	3	15
Or whatever	21	105	32	129	24	120	10	50	20	100	27	135
Or what	4	20	10	40	8	40	6	30	1	5	22	110
Or so	10	50	12	48	8	40	8	40	5	25	20	100
Or stuff (like that)	–	–	–	–	–	–	–	–	2	10	–	–
Total	133	665	220	883	289	1,445	43	215	123	615	191	955

Norm = Normalised frequencies (1,000,000 words) T = Token

Or so and *or what* perform different functions from other extenders. Overstreet (1999: 93) analysed *or what* as a general intensifier similar to *and everything* 'that can function as an intensifier'. In my data it was above all frequent in Singapore English. *Or so* was special-ised to uses with measure phrases (*a week or so*).

The highest number of *or*-extenders is found in Australian English followed by Singapore English and American English. *Or something* (and *or anything*) co-occurred with *like that* in all the varieties. *Or whatever* was slightly more frequent than *or something* in ICE-CAN.

Or something was more frequent than the long form in all varieties. *Or anything like that* was more frequent in Canadian English but the number of examples is small.

The four most frequent *and*- and *or*- extenders are shown in Table 4.7. Both *and* and *or* extenders are represented among the most frequent items in all varieties. However, there are also differences between the varieties.[15]

Table 4.7 The ranking of the four most frequent extenders in rank order in ICE-GB, SBC, ICE-AUS, ICE-CAN, ICE-NZ and ICE-SIN

ICE-GB	SBC[16]	ICE-AUS	ICE-CAN	ICE-NZ	ICE-SIN
Or something	Or something	Or something	Or whatever	And stuff	And all that
And things	And stuff	And stuff	And so on	And that	Or something
And stuff	And everything	And everything	Or something	Or something	Or something like that
Or anything	Or whatever	Or anything	Or something like that	And things	Or whatever

Or something was ranked highest in ICE-GB, SBC and ICE-AUS. In ICE-CAN *or what-ever* was more frequent than *or something*. *And stuff* was most frequent in ICE-NZ and *and all that* in ICE-SIN. *And that* was only found among the top four in ICE-NZ. The frequency of *and everything* was striking in American and Australian English. The dif-ferences between the varieties are striking. However, the rank order of the most frequent general extenders in SBC and ICE-AUS is similar.

4.6 Factors accounting for variability of general extenders

The variability of general extenders has been discussed from many different perspec-tives. The present study is synchronic only. However, grammaticalisation lurks in the background and we need to consider the relationship between formal variation and grammaticalisation. Another factor has to do with the specific functions of *and*- and *or*-extenders. However, the focus of the discussion below will be on describing the variability of the general extenders in terms of their association with politeness norms favoured by different regional varieties. General extenders can also have a real-time processing func-tion. They can function as fillers used as stallers for time especially by speakers of English as a second language.

4.6.1 Grammaticalisation

Variation within a single language has generally been analysed in terms of grammaticali-sation and semantic and pragmatic change. Grammaticalisation must also be considered as a factor behind the variation in regional varieties of English. It has been suggested that the variation between different forms of general extenders can be explained by grammaticalisation processes such as phonetic reduction (variation between short and long forms), loss of syntactic properties (decategorisation), semantic and pragmatic changes (Cheshire 2007; Pichler and Levey 2011; Tagliamonte and Denis 2010).We can distinguish more or less grammaticalised forms or what Pichler and Levey (2011: 462) describe as reflexes of 'incomplete or asynchronous grammaticalization'.

As a result of decategorisation the general noun (*things* or *stuff*) contained in the general extender loses some of its properties and is only loosely connected with the utterance in which it is integrated. In the following example the interpretation of *and things* is predictable or 'correct' because there is a noun to which the extender anaphorically refers:

(1) uh hansoms and chaises <u>and things</u>
     (ICE-GB S1A-006 #223)

'Chaises' shares features such as 'count' and 'plural' with the co-ordinated extender. In this example hansoms and chaises are presented as members of a category which is only implicated (vehicles).

The next example is less straightforward:

(2) And uh whenever you went and stayed in hotels abroad <u>and things</u> you know he'd be worrying about whether the tissue box was on the right side of the bed
     (S1A-010 #258)

And things can refer either to hotels or (more likely) to the whole clause (you went and stayed at hotels) or to the verb phrase only (stayed at hotels).

And stuff is used without any (grammatical) connection to the sentence it is in:

(3) and at the same <{1><[1>time</[1> they speak english <u>and stuff</u> there and so it's not important that i don't know spanish or anything <,> cos i mean there's just no way i don't think that i could go and live in colombia or something like that
     (ICE-NZ S1A-031#78:1)

Moreover, short forms can be hypothesised to be more grammaticalised than long forms. Both short and long forms are used. Grammaticalisation can explain that the short form becomes more frequent:

(4) B: Aduki beans are good with cumin <u>and things</u> <u>like that</u> <unclear-words>
     (ICE-GB S1A-055 #172:1)

(5) B: and they've sort of got rice and carrots <u>and things</u> in there
     (ICE-GB S1A-055 #158:1)

As a part of the grammaticalisation process the general extenders are also receiving inter-personal function. In example (2) the function of *and things* is to invoke shared knowledge of what it is like to stay at hotels abroad.

From a grammaticalisation perspective general extenders develop from a set-marking to interpersonal function. They generally have functions on different levels reflecting the paths of grammaticalisation:

> (6) B: Uhm people who had come back uh to
> do their to do their final years <u>and</u>
> <u>stuff like that</u> after working <u>you know</u> in
> in industries <unclear-words> which is like an an
> office with with <u>you know</u> people with drawing
> boards <u>and stuff like that</u>
> (ICE-GB S1A-034 019)

In the example above the function is not only set-marking but interpersonal. *And stuff like that* is used to establish solidarity and common references.

Extenders can be more or less grammaticalised. Cheshire found, for instance, that '*and that* and *and everything* were the most grammaticalized form followed by *or something* with *and things* and *and stuff* lagging behind' (Cheshire 2007: 155). *And that* is a completely fixed phrase:

> (7) <.>we</.> <O>voc</O> just going over that terangi kaheke <,>
> stuff <u>and that</u> and how <,> all his all his manuscripts <u>and that</u>
> have only ever been <,> um <,> <?>what's the word</?> analysed
> by like <,> jennifer curnow and agatha thornton and what's
> <voice=highpitched>that other guy's name i just <?>remembered</?>
> (ICE-NZ S1A-083 192)

Grammaticalisation can explain why general extenders such as *and things* or *or something* now have interpersonal function. However, all variation is not due to gram-maticalisation. General extenders live their own life once they have been grammatical-ised. They can, for instance, be used with new associations and gain affective or social meanings.

4.6.2 Function of *and-* and *or-* extenders

We should not lump *and-* and *or-* extenders together and treat them as a unitary phenom-enon. They correspond to different structures and they have different functions. The dif-ferences between them have been analysed in terms of speech style. Cheshire (2007: 161) has, for instance, suggested that informal chat in general prefers disjunctives and that the *and*-extender may be more formal. The American and especially the Australian English varieties would thus prefer a more informal style.

Moreover, *and-* and *or-* extenders can have specific functions in the interaction. *And*-extenders would be used when it is important to stress in-group membership and social similarity. *Or*-extenders on the other hand convey vagueness and have functions as hedges. A more widespread use of the *and*-extender may then suggest that positive politeness is more favoured by speakers of that variety than negative politeness.

4.6.3 Shared knowledge and positive politeness

As a discourse feature the general extender implies shared knowledge and co-operation between the speaker and the hearer. According to Evison et al. (2007: 141) general extenders 'invite the interlocutor to enter a conceptual space with the speaker where phenomena perceived as sharing characteristics are bundled together in acts of meaning-making'. Consider the following example where 'frankfurters' and 'sausages' have been bundled together:

>   (8) B: I also picked up some tins of uh *cassoulet* <,> and <,> *choucroute royale* <,>
>   that's a cabbage thing oh yes mm with <u>frankfurter and sausages</u> <u>and things</u>
>   A mm that's right (ICE-GB S1A-009 #065–069)

And things is closely associated with 'there is more'. The speaker refers to frankfurter and sausages and (more) things. The category 'in the air' is not lexicalised but must be 'within the range of shared knowledge' (O'Keeffe 2006: 129). Speaker A has picked up some tins of 'cassoulet' and 'choucroute'. Choucroute royale contains frankfurters and sausages and other ingredients which it would be over-ambitious or superfluous to enumerate. The vague category 'and things' is the result of co-operation between speakers B and A as indicated by the fact that B signals her understanding of what is referred to (*mm that's right*).

Depending on how well the speakers know each other the manoeuvring space for interpreting the reference of the extender can be more or less restricted and of different types. 'The closer the speaker relationship within the participation framework . . . the greater the shared space they can exploit' (Evison et al. 2007: 146).

It is because of their close relationship that speakers can exploit the social space to mean more than what is actually said. *And stuff* in the request 'can you buy some milk and stuff' is understood not because it refers back to 'milk' in the same utterance but because it is addressed by wife to husband. *And stuff* provides a shortcut in the conversation exploited by the speakers who know each other and each other's behaviour well. The function of *and stuff* further underlines that the speaker and the hearer have a close relationship.

And stuff is a powerful marker of intimacy based on shared feelings or experiences. The participants A and B are looking at a postcard representing a castle evoking country life symbolised by flowers, a garland and cheerfulness.

>   (9) B: There's flowers and cheerfulness and garlands <u>and all sorts of things</u>
>   I like the idea of the castle
>   A: mm <,,> country life repose concord harmony prosperity peace
>   (ICE-GB S1A 067 #299–301)

A shows that she accepts B's description of the postcard and the feelings it evokes (*mm country life concord, repose, harmony and peace*).

By referring to knowledge which is restricted to a particular group and excludes others the speaker can further reduce the distance between the speakers. The function of *and stuff* is to consolidate the close relationship among those who are familiar with the sandwich shop Tamara. Both the current speaker and the other participants co-operate in order to anchor the understanding of *and stuff*. Lenore for example has to ask whether Tamara is the shop on Hollywood (Avenue).

(10) .. [(H) And there's] all those little shops,
      JOANNE: [Unhunh].
      KEN: there's like Tamara='s,
      that sandwich shop,
      JOANNE: (TSK)
      KEN: and stuff?
      (H)=
      LENORE: On [Hollywood]?
      KEN: [U=m],
      (Santa Barbara Corpus)

The function of *and stuff* is not (only) to draw attention to those little shops like Tamara but to establish familiarity, similarity and solidarity (you and I are members of group with a local knowledge of the neighbourhood).

Further support for the use of general extenders to refer to shared knowledge rather than lexical knowledge comes from the corpus of Singapore English. Speaker A wants to know who Ge Lan is. B refers to the presumably shared knowledge that he was a star when there was a Ling Chui instead of being more specific about the time.

(11) A: Ya who's Ge Lan huh
      B: Ge Lan was uhm a star you know during the time when there was
      a Ling Chui and all that
      (ICE-SIN S1A-025#190:1)

The number of individuals who can understand this reference is probably restricted to speakers of Singapore English who can evoke certain associations from the mention of Ling Chui. Such examples are evidence of the use of general extenders to reach out to shared knowledge or experiences in order to signal rapport. What the examples have in common is that they have the function of establishing common ground and solidarity by avoiding explicitness.

Similarly, in the following example from ICE-AUS the speaker refers to places like the Regency Hotel in Melbourne as shared knowledge in order to create intimacy between the participants:

(12) The uh Park-Hyatt Coolum and places like that Regency in Melbourne and things like that (ICE-AUS S1A-018 (B):67)

The collocation with *you know* can make it clear that the extender has the function 'you know what I mean', 'I don't have to tell you everything since we are closely related'. In example (13) from the American corpus, 'Lynne' describes how one learns to mend horse shoes. *And stuff* and *you know* support each other in the broad function of invoking shared knowledge in order to create solidarity. It does not matter whether the knowledge about mending horse shoes is actually shared.

> (13) LYNNE: (H) We start out,
> (H) .. with,
> .. dead horse hooves.
> (H)= I mean,
> <X the% X> the canneries,
> <u>you know and stuff you know</u>=?
> .. The people that --
> (H)= ... that --
> .. kill the horses <u>for meat and stuff?</u>
> <u>.. You know</u> they have all these le=gs <u>and stuff?</u>
> (Santa Barbara Corpus)

Overstreet (1999: 102, quoting Macaulay 1985: 115) describes *and stuff* and *and that* as 'a kind of punctuation feature, almost the oral equivalent of a comma or a full stop dependent on intonation'. Instead of a set-marking function, *and things* is used to mark shared knowledge.

> (14) A: and um so <.>she's</.> <O>tut</O> has a lot of problems getting around <u>and things</u> and the next one had <.>a</.> major problems with drugs and she spent a lot of time in psychiatric wards <u>and things</u> and she now has a three year old child
> (ICE-NZ S1A-040# 172–173)

As a punctuation marker *and things* or *and stuff* may be repeated when a pause is needed for planning:

> (15) With with people performing <u>and stuff</u> Soon after this they started bringing in members of the the um the um A Australian Symphony Orchestra <u>and stuff</u> to play but at the time it was an amateur production
> (ICE-AUS S1A-019(B):151)

And that can be regarded as a functional equivalent of *and stuff* and *and things*. According to Pichler and Levey (2011: 444) *and that* is more frequent in UK varieties (than *and stuff*). However, its use is constrained by sociolinguistic features such as sex and socioeconomic class. However, its high frequency in British English is mainly associated with working-class speech (Cheshire 2007). In my sample it was only used by Australian and New Zealand speakers.[17] However, it was less frequent than *and stuff*. It is possible that its frequency in these variants is also associated with working-class speakers. In the New Zealand corpus it was for instance used by service station attendants, mechanics, shop owners, car salesmen and fire fighters. Thirteen out of 48 speakers were Maori speakers.[18]

4.6.4 Intensification

And everything is typically used as an intensifier, to emphasise or highlight a previous part of an assertion or question' (Overstreet 1999: 146). The intensifying or exaggerative use is a feature of involvement and positive politeness, In (16) the speaker has added *and everything* in order to increase the interest of the story by making it more dramatic:

(16) . . . and I call her and ask her how her day was <u>and everything</u>.
      FRED: ... Yeah.
      .. (H) .. What,
      what does uh,
      .. your ... sisters say.
      RICHARD: ... N- they tell me to stay away from her,
      don't even call or anything.
      FRED: ... Yeah[=]?
      RICHARD: [Wait] till she calls you <u>and everything.</u>
      (Santa Barbara Corpus)

A striking thing about Singapore English is the frequency of *and all that* in comparison with *and stuff* as a marker of shared knowledge and solidarity. We can describe *and all that* as a 'statistical' ethnic marker which is closely associated with Singaporean identity (cf. above Section 4.5). Its function is to express positive politeness, emphasis and rapport. Like *and things* it is closely associated with sharing knowledge which can be of a local kind. Both speakers are familiar with the heavy rains which are beyond control:

(17) B: I'm I'm I'm very seldom late
      C: Precisely
      B: Only during uh certain circumstances only beyond my control
      the rain <u>and all that</u>
      (ICE-SIN S1A-023#185–187)

The interpretation of *and all that* is clear to both speakers as is obvious from the fact that speaker A is able to fill in the gap ('dark soya sauce' in example 18). The speakers are discussing what goes into a Cantonese dish called mango beef:

(18) A: Uhm you don't use so much oyster sauce you use a bit more uhm
      all sorts of things
      B: Yep Wine <u>and all that</u>
      A: Dark dark soya sauce
      (ICE-SIN S1A-019#214–217)

Extenders such as 'and all that shit' are not only 'affective-rapport conveying' (Terraschke and Holmes 2007: 108) but signal a negative attitude to what is said (eating glop as fish do).

(19) (TSK) (H) He drops the goldfish into the tank,
      and the goldfish goes and sw- swims around,

> minding his own little business,
> eating glop <u>and all that shit,</u>
> you know,
> that fish do,
> (Santa Barbara Corpus)

Or anything is functionally related to *and everything* but occurs primarily in negative sentences. It is used to emphasise what is claimed in the preceding sentence:

    (20) She was never in any of my classes <u>or anything</u>
          (S1A-050(B):247)

4.6.5 Hedging and negative politeness

The *or*-extender involves a different discourse style and different social norms. Overstreet (1999: 147) describes the discourse function of *or something* as hedging:

> Typically used as a hedge to mark the content of an assertion as possibly inaccurate, or approximate . . . Also found in invitations, offers, proposals, and requests, where it is used to indicate alternative options, and to express tentativeness (a strategy of negative politeness).

In (21) *or something* is used in an offer or invitation with a face-threat mitigating force. It co-occurs with other mitigating markers such as the 'polite' *could*.

    (21) B: We could have dinner that evening <u>or something</u>
          (ICE-GB S1A-005 #087)

Or something can also mark the content of the assertion as 'possibly inaccurate' (Overstreet 1999: 147). In example (22) it is implied that an argument might not be the right word.

    (22) D: there might have been an argument <u>or something</u> but i i never
          thought that they would try and stop me
          (ICE-NZ S1B-070#135:1)

Another possible interpretation is that *or something* conveys to the hearer that the topic is embarrassing.

    In all varieties a frequent meaning of *or something* (or *or so*) was to express approximation with count words:

    (23) Let's just say it's nine cents <u>or something</u>
          (ICE-AUS S1A-006(B):305)

Or whatever was slightly more frequent than *or something* in ICE-CAN but in the other varieties it was not as frequent as *or something*. According to Overstreet (1999) it can mark indifference, an attitude of 'I don't care'. It was frequent in Australian English but not as frequent as *or something*. However, it is often difficult to distinguish functionally from *or something*.

4.6.6 General extenders and fluency

Speakers of English as a second-language variety may find it more difficult than native speakers to produce language under the pressure of the constraints imposed by real-time processing. According to Gilquin (2008: 141),

> This is because, next to the question of what to say ('conceptualization') speakers have to work out how to say it ('formulation') and given that the language in which learners express themselves is not their mother tongue but a – usually imperfectly acquired – foreign or second language, this second step normally involves more difficulties for them than native speakers.

General extenders are used to 'buy' the speaker some time for formulating what to say and in addition can give an impression of fluency. We may expect that speakers of Singapore English and New Zealand England find them useful as stalling devices and to hold the turn when they speak English while the speakers represented in the ICE-GB or ICE-CAN avoid them as 'uneducated'.

4.7 Conclusion

Pragmatic markers have been described by Mair as 'a fragile area in the linguistic system' (2009: 10). General extenders are characterised by formal and functional variability. The hypothesis underlying this study is that it is not sufficient to study their use and variation in British English but we need to take a global perspective and consider other 'World Englishes'. In this study I have therefore looked at the influence of the regional variety of English on the choice of particular variants of the general extender. The corpora have been useful in showing that the general extenders are differently distributed in the varieties studied and that there are differences in the general frequencies with which they are found. A number of explanations for the distributional variation have been proposed. For example, the variation can be explained against the backdrop of grammaticalisation processes and their interaction with social and regional factors. Especially in varieties where the speakers (or some speakers) use English as a second language general extenders are linked to aspects of fluency. They can help the speaker to reduce the pressure imposed by the need to plan ahead while simultaneously executing the message.

Varieties may also be kept apart by different cultural habits as regards politeness or speech style and co-operative principles (be brief, don't say something unnecessary). The principles underlying the use of general extenders are 'of a social sort' (Brown and Levinson 1977: 61) and involve strategies of positive and negative politeness. Positive politeness answers human needs for intimacy, solidarity, membership of the group and negative politeness strategies respond to threats to the speaker's face.

The *and*-extender is closely associated with 'there is more' (Overstreet 1999) and is used by the speaker to invite the hearer to share knowledge or experience. As we have seen above, *and*-extenders are a way of making it explicit that the speaker and hearer share familiarity with local customs and values as well as knowledge about places and people. They can therefore also be used to create 'a social space' beyond what is actually said when knowledge is not shared. The reference to knowledge which is shared by a social group or by speakers sharing a regional identity has the function of drawing the speaker and the hearer closer together and can create solidarity within the group. *And*-extenders fit in well with face-enhancing and positive politeness, unlike the *or*-extenders which are characterised by distancing, hedging and lack of involvement (strategies of negative politeness).

There is considerable variation between individual forms in different varieties. *And stuff* is common in American, Australian and New Zealand English. The counterpart in British English is *and things* (although the change to *and stuff* may be spreading). When a certain variant is particularly frequent in a particular variant it can acquire social significance as a marker of ethnic identity in addition to its other functions. *And that* is for instance such a statistical regionalism characterising New Zealand and Australian English. In Singapore English *and all that* can be regarded as a stereotypical solidarity marker.

This study should be considered only as a first step in exploring the possibility of studying general extenders (and other spoken phenomena) in the context of English as a world language on the basis of the ICE-corpora. It would be interesting to add other ICE-varieties in order to study common tendencies in 'Englishes' which have become independent varieties (e.g. Hong Kong English, Indian English, Jamaican English). We also need to find out more about the interaction of general extenders with social and cultural factors in different regional varieties. Sociolinguistic factors such as age, class and gender have been shown to be important in British English and can be assumed to explain the variability of general extenders in other regional varieties as well.

Notes

1. Aijmer (2002) referred to them as 'particles with vague reference'. Other terms are for example 'set-marking tags' (Dines 1980), 'coordination tags' (Biber et al. 1999), 'discourse extenders' (Norrby and Winter 2002), 'vague category marker' (O'Keeffe 2004).
2. As shown in later research the term 'set-marking tag' is problematic since it suggests that the preceding phrase is (always) a member of the set.
3. Compare also Terraschke (2007) for rules describing the variation of *and-* and *or-*extenders in New Zealand English in the form of a construction map.
4. We also find examples with other nouns. Compare for example: 'David Smith and Mike Steward and all these dudes' (ICE-NZ) and 'you take Michelin and all those sort of names' (ICE-NZ).
5. The construction also allows an adjective before the noun. Compare, for example: 'and all those kind of yummy things' (ICE-NZ).
6. The ICE corpora are representative of many different spoken and written genres. It would therefore be possible to describe their use in public dialogue for example in classroom lessons or in press news reportage or editorials.
7. Holmes (1996) discusses the problems of defining 'what is a New Zealander' and how to represent both Maori Speakers and 'Pakeha' speakers (a non-Maori speaker

usually of European origin) in the New Zealand Component of the ICE Corpus. The goal was that approximately 12 per cent of the speakers should be Maori. However, we do not have a similar discussion of who the speakers are for the other varieties.

8. The Santa Barbara Corpus (SBC) 'represents a wide variety of people of different regional origins, ages, occupations, genders, and ethnic and social backgrounds' (quoted from http://www.linguistics.ucsb.edu/research/sbcorpus.html [accessed 4 October 2012]). The corpus consists of 60 discourse segments. They represent conversations among family members or close friends but also task-related conversations, lectures, sermons, business conversations and medical interactions. This should be kept in mind when we compare American English with the other varieties.

9. Because of the size and number of corpora studied it has not been possible to use a bottom-up approach to identify all the general extenders. O'Keeffe (2004) on the other hand used a small corpus of radio phone-in shows and was able to collect 'vague categories' manually. 'The benefit of this bottom-up approach is that we have been able to identify all of the vague categories in the data as well as all of the forms used to construct them in this specific context' (O'Keeffe 2004: 19).

10. Tagliamonte and Denis, on the other hand, found a large number of general extenders in the the Toronto English Archive (TEA). The data represent 87 speakers strategically selected to represent a sample balanced by age and sex (2010: 346). The ICE-CAN corpus is much smaller and is not socially stratified by age or sex.

11. The most frequent noun was *shit* (or *bullshit*), especially American English. Compare also *and all the rest, and all that rubbish, and all that crap, and all that nonsense, and all that jazz.*

12. Compare Dines's (1980) data from Australian English where *and things* was more frequent than *and stuff.*

13. Long forms with *and everything (and everything like that)* were infrequent and have not been included.

14. Or 8 variants if we include *or stuff (like that)* occurring twice in New Zealand English.

15. Biber et al. (1999: 116) have discussed what they refer to as co-ordination tags (based on the Longman Spoken and Written English Corpus). Their rank ordering is 1. *Or something* 2. *And everything* 3. *And things* 4. *And stuff (like that)*. However, they do not distinguish between British and American English. On the other hand they point out that some co-ordination tags are less frequent in conversation than in other registers. Both *and so on* and *etc.* are, for instance, typical of academic prose and *or so* is more characteristic of fiction than of conversation.

16. Overstreet (1999) also found that the most frequently used general extenders in her American corpus of telephone and face-to-face conversation were *or something* and *and stuff* in that order.

17. Compare, however, Pichler and Levey (2011: 444), 'Overall, *and that* is strongly associated with New Zealand and British English varieties'.

18. No information was available about the Australian speakers.

5

Conclusion

Pragmatic markers vary according to a large number of factors. In variational pragmatics the focus has been factors such as social class, ethnicity, gender and age. In this work I have taken a different route and considered pragmatic markers in different spoken text types and situations. We can assume that these factors play an important role although they have so far not been integrated into variational pragmatics: 'At present, it is not sufficiently clear how further relevant concepts can be fruitfully integrated into the current framework of variational pragmatics. Such concepts include genres, registers, styles, activity types, communities of practice, and relational work' (cf. Schneider 2007; Haugh and Schneider 2012; Schneider 2010: 250).

Chapters 2 to 4 have dealt with the variability of some selected pragmatic markers in text types, activities, speech and writing and to some extent in different national standards. There is, for example, a close relationship between text type and conditions on what is appropriate or polite to say in a certain situation. In the last chapter the perspective is widened to take into account cultural and social differences as evidenced in different regional varieties of English. This is a neglected area in the study of pragmatic markers and a gap which can be filled by the availability of corpora of national varieties of English which can be compared with each other.

The pragmatic markers discussed in this work have been chosen because of their multifunctionality and variability. *Well,* in particular, is notorious for its multifunctionality. However, its meanings are related to each other by polysemy and more weakly by indexicality. We can distinguish core meanings which can be the source for a number of sub-senses. The aim of this study has also been to show that *well* (and other pragmatic markers) has text-type specific functions resulting from the 'stretching' or 'modification' of an already existing meaning. In order to describe the differences between the varieties we need to refer to interpretative frames, for example, to 'the classroom frame' which specifies the roles of the teacher and the pupils and specific functions associated with the activity such as the transition from one stage in the lesson to another.

There is a close relationship between the form of pragmatic markers and their functions although the relationship is complex and often involves frequencies. There is, for instance, a link between position and function which is exploited by the speaker to get his or her meaning across. However, position is also related to other factors such as speech or writing and to text type.

Actually and *in fact* can be assumed to have a similar meaning potential since they share core meanings (associated with adversativity and elaboration). However, they are typical of different text types and have not developed the same sub-senses or contextual functions. *Actually* is more flexible than *in fact*, that is, it has a number of functions which are not shared by *in fact* and can be explained by the text type where it is most frequent. It occurs, for example, in conversation with functions such as self-repair or to shift the topic in the conversation. Moreover, *actually* and *in fact* do not have the same specialised meanings or the same connotations. *In fact* is more likely than *actually* to assume indexical meanings such as authority and knowledgeability while *actually* sounds apologetic and is associated with politeness.

The last chapter on general extenders differs from the chapters on *well* and on *actually* and *in fact* in that the pragmatic markers are investigated in a number of national varieties of English (rather than in different text types). The differences between the varieties are discussed in terms of the cultural conventions and norms of politeness for what is appropriate in a particular society. However, a variety of factors may be needed to explain the differences. We need, for example, to consider the constraints imposed by real-time processing on fluency. Speakers of English as a second-language variety may find it more difficult to formulate what they want to say than native speakers and therefore use general extenders more frequently than native speakers of English and for different reasons.

In the way of conclusion I want to return to 'larger issues' and discuss what can be learnt about meaning and multifunctionality by studying pragmatic markers in a variational perspective.

Pragmatic markers do not have a stable meaning but a meaning potential, that is, a rich meaning representation where the meanings are related to each other in different ways. By studying the markers in many different text types and activities and with different speakers we can get a better picture of what the potential functions, sub-senses and collocations are, how they are derived from core meanings and of the role of the literal meaning. The meaning potential is a fairly abstract representation of the speaker's knowledge about the meanings of a particular pragmatic marker which should also be able to describe its indexical ties to a particular activity. The meaning potential of a pragmatic marker would by its nature not be complete although it consists of a specifiable set of formal and functional features. A problem has been to explain how language users can interpret innovative uses of the pragmatic markers without too much effort. The existence of a meaning potential suggests a dynamic theory of meaning building where speakers use existing meanings in creative ways in order to fit them into situations which the speaker has not encountered before.

A distinction needs to be made between the meaning potential or a fairly abstract representation of how a pragmatic marker is used and the actual use of pragmatic markers in communication. In the actual communication situation the function of a pragmatic marker is constrained by the meaning potential although the speaker can also use the marker for unusual, innovative or manipulative purposes. A particular function is selected along with formal features such as position, prosody or collocations associated with a text type, a social situation and particular stages of the interaction.

References

Aijmer, K. 2002. *English Discourse Particles: Evidence from a Corpus*. Amsterdam and Philadelphia: John Benjamins.

Aijmer, K. 2011. '*Well I'm not sure I think* . . .: The use of *well* by non-native speakers'. *International Journal of Corpus Linguistics* 16(2): 231–54.

Aijmer, K., A. Foolen and A-.M. Simon-Vandenbergen. 2006. 'Pragmatic markers in translation: A methodological proposal'. In K. Fischer (ed.), *Approaches to Discourse Particles*. Amsterdam: Elsevier. 101–14.

Aijmer, K. and A.-M. Simon-Vandenbergen. 2003. '*Well* in English, Swedish and Dutch'. *Linguistics* 41(6): 1123–61.

Allwood, J. J. Nivre and E. Ahlsén. 1990. 'Speech management: on the non-written life of speech'. *Nordic Journal of Linguistics* 13: 3–48.

Altenberg, B. 1987. *Prosodic Patterns in Spoken English: Studies in the Correlation between Prosody and Grammar for Text-to-Speech Conversion*. Lund Studies in English 76: Lund University Press.

Andersen, G. 2001. *Pragmatic Markers and Sociolinguistic Variation*. Amsterdam and Philadelphia: John Benjamins.

Andersen, E., M. Brizuela, B. DuPuy, and L. Gonnerman. 1999. 'Cross-linguistic evidence for the acquisition of discourse markers as register variables'. *Journal of Pragmatics* 31: 1339–51.

Barron, A. and K. Schneider. 2009. 'Variational pragmatics: Studying the impact of social factors on language use in interaction'. *Intercultural Pragmatics* 6(4): 425–42.

Bazzanella, C. 2006. 'Discourse markers in Italian: Towards a "compositional" meaning'. In K. Fischer (ed.), *Approaches to Discourse Particles*. Amsterdam: Elsevier. 449–64.

Beeching, K. 2010. 'Semantic change: Evidence from false friends.' *Languages in Contrast* 10(2): 139–65.

Biber, D. and E. Finegan. 1988. 'Adverbial stance types in English'. *Discourse Processes* 11: 1–34.

—1989. 'Styles of stance in English: Lexical and grammatical marking of evidentiality and affect'. *Text* 9: 93–124.

Biber, D., S. Johansson, G. Leech, S. Conrad and E. Finegan. 1999. *The Longman Grammar of Spoken and Written English*. London: Longman.

Blakemore, D. 2002. *Relevance and Linguistic Meaning: The Semantics and Pragmatics of Discourse Markers*. Cambridge: Cambridge University Press.

Bolinger, D. 1989. *Intonation and its Uses: Melody in Grammar and Discourse*. London: Edward Arnold.

Brinton, L. J. 1996. *Pragmatic Markers in English: Grammaticalization and Discourse Functions*. Berlin: Mouton de Gruyter.

—2008. *The Comment Clause in English: Syntactic Origin and Pragmatic Development*. Cambridge: Cambridge University Press.

Britain, D. 1992. 'Linguistic change in intonation: The use of high rising terminals in New Zealand English'. *Language Variation and Change*. 4: 77–104.

Brown, P. and S. Levinson. 1977. 'Universals in language usage: Politeness phenomena'. In E. Goody (ed.), *Questions and Politeness: Strategies in Social Interaction*. Cambridge: Cambridge University Press. 56–310.

Bruti, S. 1999. '*In fact* and *infatti*: The same, similar or different'. *Pragmatics* 9(4): 519–33.

Carlson, L. 1984. '*Well' in Dialogue Games: A Discourse Analysis of the Interjection 'Well' in Idealized Conversation*. Amsterdam and Philadelphia: John Benjamins.

Carter, R. and M. McCarthy. 2006. *The Cambridge Grammar of English*. Cambridge: Cambridge University Press.

Cheng, W. 2007. 'The use of vague language across spoken genres in an intercultural Hong Kong Corpus'. In J. Cutting (ed.), *Vague Language Explored*. Basingstoke: Palgrave Macmillan. 161–81.

Cheshire, J. 2007. 'Discourse variation, grammaticalization and stuff like that'. *Journal of Sociolinguistics*. 11(2): 155–93. http://www.uwa.edu.au/LingWWW/als99/proceedings.html (accessed 4 October 2012).

Clift, R. 2001. 'Meaning in interaction: The case of *actually*'. *Language* 77(2): 245–91.

Columbus, G. 1999. 'A corpus-based analysis of invariant tags in five varieties of English'. In A. Renouf and A. Kehoe (eds), *Corpus Linguistics: Refinements and Reassessments*. Amsterdam and New York: Rodopi. 401–14.

Cuenca, M.-J. 2008. 'Pragmatic markers in contrast: The case of *well*'. *Journal of Pragmatics* (40) 8, 1373–91.

De Fina, A. 1997. 'An analysis of Spanish *bien* as a marker of classroom management in teacher-student interaction'. *Journal of Pragmatics* 28: 337–54.

de Klerk, V. 2005. 'Procedural meanings of *well* in a corpus of Xhosa English'. *Journal of Pragmatics* 37: 1183–205.

Defour, T. 2009. '*Well, well! What a surprise!* A diachronic look at the relation between *well, well* and the pragmatic marker *well*'. In S. Slembrouck, M. Taverniers and M. Van Herreweghe (eds), *From 'Will' to 'Well': Studies in Linguistics Offered to Anne-Marie Simon-Vandenbergen*. Gent: Academia Press. 161–72.

Defour, T., U. D'Hondt, A.-M. Simon-Vandenbergen. 2010. 'Degrees of pragmaticalization: The divergent histories of *actually* and *actuellement*'. *Languages in Contrast* 10(2): 166–93.

Deppermann, A. 2006. *Construction Grammar* – eine Grammatik für die Interaktion? In

A. Depperman, R. Fiehler and T. Spranz-Fogasy (eds), *Grammatik und Interaktion*. Radolphzell: Verlag für Gespraechsforschung. 43–66.

Dines, E. R. 1980. 'Variation in discourse "and stuff like that"'. *Language in Society* 9: 13–33.

Dorr-Bremme, D. W. 1990. 'Contextualization cues in the classroom'. *Language in Society* 19: 379–402.

Du Bois, J., W. Schuetze-Coburn, S. Cumming and D. Paolino. 1993. 'Outline of discourse transcription'. In J. A. Edwards and M. D. Lampert (eds), *Talking data: Transcription and Coding in Discourse Research*. Hillsdale, NJ: Lawrence Erlbaum Associates. 33–43.

Evison, J., M. McCarthy and A. O'Keeffe. 2007. '"Looking out for love and all the rest of it": Vague category markers as shared social space'. In J. Cutting (ed.), *Vague Language Explored*. Basingstoke: Palgrave Macmillan. 138–57.

Ferrara, K. 1997. 'Form and function of the discourse marker *anyway:* Implications for discourse analysis'. *Linguistics* 35: 345–78.

Fischer, K. 2000. *From Cognitive Semantics to Lexical Pragmatics: The Functional Polysemy of Discourse Particles*. Berlin: Mouton de Gruyter.

—(ed.), 2006. *Approaches to Discourse Particles*. Amsterdam: Elsevier.

Fraser, B. 1996. 'Pragmatic markers'. *Pragmatics*: 167–90.

Fraser, B. and M. Malamud-Makowski. 1996. English and Spanish contrastive markers. *Language Sciences* 18: 863–81.

Fried, M and J.-O. Östman. 2005. 'Construction grammar and spoken language: The case of pragmatic particles'. *Journal of Pragmatics* 37: 1752–78.

Fuller, M. 2003. 'The influence of speaker roles on discourse marker use'. *Journal of Pragmatics* 35: 23–45.

García Vizcaíno, M. J. and M. A. Martínez-Cabeza. 2005. 'The pragmatics of *well* and *bueno* in English and Spanish'. *Intercultural Pragmatics* 2(3): 69–92.

Gilquin, G. 2008. 'Hesitation markers among EFL learners: Pragmatic deficiency or difference?' In J. Romero-Trillo (ed.), *Corpus and Pragmatics: A Mutualistic Entente*. Berlin and New York: Mouton de Gruyter. 119–49.

Goodwin, M. H. 1990. *He-Said-She-Said: Talk As Social Organization Among Black Children*. Bloomington: Indiana University Press.

Greasley, P. 1994. 'An investigation into the use of the particle *well*: Commentaries on a game of snooker'. *Journal of Pragmatics* 22: 477–94.

Green, G. 2006. 'Discourse particles and the symbiosis of natural language processing and basic research'. In B. Birner (ed.), *Drawing the Boundaries of Meaning: Neo-Gricean Studies in Pragmatics and Semantics in Honor of Laurence R. Horn*. Amsterdam: John Benjamins. 117–35.

Grice, H. P. 1975. 'Logic and conversation'. In P. Cole and J. L. Morgan (eds), *Syntax and Semantics, Vol. 9, Pragmatics*. New York: Academic Press.

Gumperz, J. J. 1996. 'The linguistic and cultural relativity of inference'. In J. J. Gumperz, and S. C. Levinson (eds), *Rethinking Linguistic Relativity*. Cambridge: Cambridge University Press. 374–406.

Gumperz, J. J. and S. C. Levinson (eds), 1996. *Rethinking linguistic relativity*. Cambridge: Cambridge University Press.

Hale, S. 1999. 'Interpreters' treatment of discourse markers in courtroom questions'. *Forensic Linguistics* 6: 57–82.

Halliday, M. A. K. and R. Hasan. 1976. *Cohesion in English*. London: Longman.

Harris, S. 1980. *Language Interaction in Magistrates' Courts*. Unpublished PhD thesis, University of Nottingham.

Haugh, M. and Schneider, Klaus P. 2012. 'Impoliteness across Englishes'. *Journal of Pragmatics* 44(9): 1017–21.

Haviland, J. B. 1987. 'Fighting words: evidential particles, affect and argument'. *Proceedings of the Berkeley Linguistics Society* 13. 'Parasession on grammar and cognition', edited by J. Aske, N. Berry, L. Michaelis and H. Filip. Berkeley: Berkeley Linguistics Society. 343–54.

—1989. 'Sure, sure: evidence and affect'. Special issue on 'Discourse and Affect', ed. E. Ochs and B. Schieffelin. *Text* 9(1): 27–68.

—1996. 'Language form and communicative practices'. In J. J. Gumperz and S. C. Levinson (eds), *Rethinking Linguistic Relativity*. Cambridge: Cambridge University Press. 271–323.

Hickey, L. 1991. 'Surprise, surprise, but do so politely'. *Journal of Pragmatics* 15: 367–72.

Hirschberg, J. and D. Litman. 1993. 'Empirical studies on disambiguation of cue phrases'. *Computational Linguistics* 19: 501–30.

Holmes, J. 1986. 'Functions of *you know* in women's and men's speech'. *Language in Society* 15: 1–22.

—1988a. '*Of course*: A pragmatic particle in New Zealand women's and men's speech'. *Australian Journal of Linguistics* 8: 49–74.

—1988b. '*Sort of* in New Zealand women's and men's speech'. *Studia Linguistica* 42: 85–121.

—1990. 'Hedges and boosters in women's and men's speech'. *Language and Communication* 10(3): 185–205.

—1996. 'The New Zealand spoken component of ICE: Some methodological challenges'. In S. Greenbaum (ed.), *Comparing English Worldwide: The International Corpus of English*. Oxford: Clarendon Press. 163–81.

Horne, M., P. Hansson, G. Bruce, J. Frid and M. Filipsson. 2001. 'Cue words and the topic structure of spoken discourse: The case of Swedish *men*'. *Journal of Pragmatics* 33: 1061–81.

Hymes, D. 1972. 'Models of the interaction of language and social life'. In J. J. Gumperz and D. Hymes (eds), *Directions in Sociolinguistics: The Ethnography of Communication*. New York: Holt, Rinehart and Winston. 35–71.

Imo, W. 2009. 'Where does the mountain stop? A granular approach to the concept of constructions-as-signs'. Place of publication unknown.

Innes, B. 2010. '"*Well*, that's why I asked the question sir": *Well* as a discourse marker in court'. *Language in Society* 39: 95–117.

Johansson, S. 2006. 'How well can *well* be translated? On the English discourse particle *well* and its correspondences in Norwegian and German'. In K. Aijmer and A.-M. Simon-Vandenbergen (eds), *Pragmatic Markers in Contrast*. Amsterdam: Elsevier. 115–37.

Jucker, A. H. 1993. 'The discourse marker *well*: A relevance theoretical account'. *Journal of Pragmatics* 19: 435–52.

Keevallik, L. 2003. *From Interaction to Grammar: Estonian Finite Verb Forms in Conversation*. Studis Uralica Upsaliensia 34. Uppsala.

Lakoff, R. 1973. 'Questionable answer and answerable questions'. In B. R. Kachru, B. Lees, Y. Malkiel et al. (eds), *Issues in Linguistics in Honor of Henry and Renée Kahane.* Urbana: University of Illinois. 453–67.

Lam, P. 2006. '*Well but that's the effect of it:* The use of *well* as a discourse particle in talk shows'. *Sprache und Datenverarbeitung* (*International Journal for Language Data Processing*) 30(1): 99–108.

—2009. 'The effect of text type on the use of *so* as a discourse particle'. *Discourse Studies* 11: 353–72.

Lenk, U. 1998. *Marking Discourse Coherence: Functions of Discourse Markers in Spoken English.* Tübingen: Gunter Narr Verlag.

Levinson, S. C. 1979. 'Activity types and language'. *Linguistics* 17: 365–79.

—1983. *Pragmatics.* Cambridge: Cambridge University Press.

Lewis, D. 2006. 'Discourse markers in English: A discourse-pragmatic view'. In Fischer, K. (ed.) *Approaches to Discourse Particles.* Amsterdam: Elsevier. 4–59.

Linell, P. 1998. *Approaching Dialogue: Talk, Interaction and Contexts in Dialogical Perspectives.* Amsterdam: John Benjamins.

—2009. *Rethinking Language, Mind and World Dialogically: Interactional and Contextual Theories of Human Sense-Making.* Charlotte, NC: Information Age Publishing.

Lucy, J. 1993. *Reflexive Language. Reported Speech and Metapragmatics.* Cambridge: Cambridge University Press.

Macaulay, R. 1985. 'The narrative skills of a Scottish coal miner'. In M. Görlach (ed.), *Focus on Scotland.* Amsterdam: John Benjamins. 101–24.

Mair, C. 2009. 'Corpus linguistics meets sociolinguistics: The role of corpus evidence in the study of sociolinguistic variation and change'. In A. Renouf and A. Kehoe (eds), *Corpus Linguistics: Refinements and Reassessments.* Amsterdam and New York: Rodopi. 7–32.

McCarthy, M. and A. O'Keeffe. 2002. 'Vague language and participation framework: Indices of identity among group, culture and nation.' Paper read at the 35th Annual Conference of the British Association for Applied Linguistics, University of Cardiff, 12–14 September 2002.

Mertz, E. and J. Yovel. 2003. 'Metalinguistic awareness'. In J Verschueren, J.-O. Östman, J. Blommaert and C. Bulcaen (eds), *Handbook of Pragmatics.* Dordrecht: Kluwer. 1–26.

Mey, J. [1993] 2001, *Pragmatics: An Introduction.* 2nd edn. Oxford: Blackwell.

Mortier, L. and L. Degand. 2009. 'Adversative discourse markers in contrast'. *International Journal of Corpus Linguistics* 14(3): 339–66

Müller, S. 2004. '*Well you know that type of person:* Functions of *well* in the speech of American and German students'. *Journal of Pragmatics* 36: 1157–82.

—2005. *Discourse Markers in Native and Non-native English Discourse.* Amsterdam and Philadelphia: John Benjamins.

Nelson, G. 1996. 'Markup systems'. In S. Greenbaum (ed.), *Comparing English Worldwide: The International Corpus of English.* Oxford: Clarendon Press. 36–53.

Norén, K. and P. Linell. 2007. 'Meaning potentials and the interaction between lexis and contexts: An empirical substantiation'. *Pragmatics* 17(3): 387–416.

Norrby, C. and J. Winter. 2002. 'Affiliation in adolescents' use of discourse extenders'. *Proceedings of the 2001 Conference of the Australian Linguistic Society.* http://www.als.asn.au/proceedings/als2001.html (accessed 22 October 2012).

Norrick, N. R. 2001. 'Discourse markers in oral narrative'. *Journal of Pragmatics* 33: 848–78.

Ochs, E. 1996. 'Linguistic resources for socializing humanity'. In J. J. Gumperz and S. C. Levinson (eds), *Rethinking Linguistic Relativity*. Cambridge: Cambridge University Press. 407–37.

Oh, S. 2000. '*Actually* and *in fact* in American English: A data-based analysis'. *English Language and Linguistics* 4(2): 243–68.

O'Keeffe, A. 2004. '"Like the wise virgins and all that jazz": Using a corpus to examine vague categorization and shared knowledge'. *Language and Computers* 52: 1–26.

—2006. *Investigating Media Discourse*. London: Routledge.

Östman, J.-O. 1995. 'Pragmatic particles twenty years after'. In B. Wårvik, S.-K. Tanskanen and R. Hiltunen (eds), *Organization in Discourse*. Turku: University of Turku. 95–108.

—2006. 'Constructions in cross-language research: Verbs as pragmatic particles in Solv'. In K. Aijmer and A.-M. Simon-Vandenbergen (eds), *Pragmatic Markers in Contrast*. Amsterdam: Elsevier. 237–57.

Overstreet, M. 1999. *Whales, Candlelight and Stuff Like That: General Extenders in English Discourse*. Oxford University Press.

Overstreet, M. and G.Yule. 1997. 'On being explicit and stuff in contemporary American English'. *Journal of English Linguistics* 25(3): 250–8.

Pichler, Heike. 2010. 'Methods in discourse variation analysis: Reflections on the way forward'. *Journal of Sociolinguistics* 14(5): 581–608.

Pichler, H. and S. Levey. 2011. 'In search of grammaticalization in synchronic dialect data: General extenders in north-east England'. *English Language and Linguistics* 15(3): 441–71.

Platt, J., H. Weber and M. L. Ho. 1984. *The New Englishes*. London: Routledge and Kegan Paul.

Pons Bordería, S. 2006. 'A functional approach to the study of discourse markers'. In K. Fischer (ed.), *Approaches to Discourse Particles*. Amsterdam: Elsevier. 77–99.

Powell, M. J. 1992. 'The systematic development of correlated interpersonal and metalinguistic uses of stance adverbs'. *Cognitive Linguistics* 3(1): 75–110.

Quirk, R., S. Greenbaum, G. Leech and J. Svartvik. 1985. *A Comprehensive Grammar of the English Language*. London: Longman.

Redeker, G. 1990. 'Ideational and pragmatic markers of discourse structure'. *Journal of Pragmatics* 14: 367–81.

—1991. 'Linguistic markers of discourse structure'. *Linguistics* 29: 1139–72.

—2006. 'Discourse markers as attentional cues at discourse transitions'. In K. Fischer (ed.), *Approaches to Discourse Particles*. Amsterdam: Elsevier. 339–58.

Romero-Trillo, J. 2002. 'The pragmatic fossilization of discourse markers in non-native speakers of English'. *Journal of Pragmatics* 34: 769–84.

Rossari, C. 1992. '*De fait, en fait, en réalité:* Trois marqueurs aux emplois inclusifs'. *Verbum* 14(3): 139–61

Rühlemann, C. 2007. *Conversation in Context: A Corpus-Driven Approach*. London and New York: Continuum.

Sapir, E. [1931] 1951. 'Communication'. In D. G. Mandelbaum (ed.), *The Selected*

Writings of Edward Sapir in Language, Culture and Personality. Berkeley and Los Angeles: University of California Press. 104–9.

Schegloff, E. 1981. 'Discourse as an interactional achievement: Some uses of "uh huh" and other things that come between sentences'. Georgetown University Round Table on Languages and Linguistics. In D. Tannen, *Analyzing Discourse: Text and Talk*. Washington, DC: Georgetown University Press. 71–93.

—1986. 'On the organization of sequences as a source of "coherence" in talk-in-interaction'. Prepared for discussion at SRCD conference on Development of Conversational Coherence, University of New Orleans, May 1986.

Schiffrin, D. 1985. 'Conversational coherence: the role of *well*'. *Language* 61: 640–67.

—1987. *Discourse Markers*. Cambridge: Cambridge University Press.

Schmied, J. 1996. 'Second-language corpora'. In S. Greenbaum (ed.), *Comparing English Worldwide: The International Corpus of English*. Oxford: Clarendon Press. 182–96.

Schneider, E. 2007. *Postcolonial English: Varieties Around the World*. Cambridge: Cambridge University Press.

Schneider, K. P. 2010. 'Variational pragmatics'. In M. Fried, J.-O. Östman and J. Verschueren (eds), *Variation and Change. Pragmatic Perspectives*. Amsterdam and Philadelphia: John Benjamins. 239–67.

Schneider, K. P. and A. Barron (eds). 2008. *Variational Pragmatics: A Focus on Regional Varieties in Pluricentric Languages*. Amsterdam and Philadelphia: John Benjamins.

Schourup, L. 1985. *Common Discourse Particles in English Conversation*. Garland: New York.

—2001. 'Rethinking *well*'. *Journal of Pragmatics* 33: 1026–60.

Schwenter, S. A. and E. C. Traugott. 2000. 'Invoking scalarity: The development of *in fact*'. *Journal of Historical Pragmatics*. 7–27.

Silverstein, M. 1992. 'Metapragmatic discourse and metapragmatic function'. In J. Lucy (ed.), *Reflexive Language*. Cambridge: Cambridge University Press. 33–58.

Simon-Vandenbergen, A-M. and D. Willems. 2011. 'Crosslinguistic data as evidence in the grammaticalization debate: The case of discourse markers'. *Linguistics* 49(2): 333–64.

Sinclair, J. McH. and R. M. Coulthard. 1975. *Towards an Analysis of Discourse: The English Used by Teachers and Pupils*. Oxford: Oxford University Press.

Smith, S. W. and A. H. Jucker. 2000. '*Actually* and other markers of an apparent discrepancy between propositional attitudes of conversational partners'. In G. Andersen and T. Fretheim (eds), *Pragmatic markers and Propositional Attitude*. Amsterdam and Philadelphia: John Benjamins. 207–37.

Stenström, A.-B. 1990a. 'Lexical items peculiar to spoken discourse'. In J. Svartvik (ed.), *The London-Lund Corpus of Spoken English: Description and Research*. Lund: Lund University Press. 137–75.

—1990b. 'Pauses in monologue and dialogue'. In J. Svartvik (ed.), *The London-Lund Corpus of Spoken English: Description and Research*. Lund: Lund University Press. 211–52.

Stenström, A.-B., G. Andersen and I. K. Hasund. 2002. *Trends in Teenage Talk*. Amsterdam and Philadelphia: John Benjamins.

Stubbe, M. and J. Holmes. 2000. 'Signalling Maori and Pakeha identity through New Zealand English discourse'. In A. Bell and K. Kuiper (eds), *New Zealand English*. Amsterdam and Philadelphia: John Benjamins. 249–78.

Stubbs, M. 1983. *Discourse Analysis: The Sociolinguistic Analysis of Natural Language.* Oxford: Blackwell.

Svartvik, J. 1980. '*Well* in conversation'. In S. Greenbaum, G. N. Leech and J. Svartvik (eds), *Studies in English Linguistics for Randolph Quirk.* London: Longman. 167–77.

Tagliamonte, S. A. and D. Denis. 2010. 'The stuff of change: General extenders in Toronto, Canada'. *Journal of English Linguistics* 38(4): 335–68.

Taglicht, J. 2001. '*Actually*, there's more to it than meets the eye'. *English Language and Linguistics* 5(1): 1–16.

Tannen, D. and C. Wallat. 1987. 'Interactive frames and knowledge schemas in interaction: Examples from a medical examination interview'. *Social Psychology Quarterly* 50: 205–16.

Terraschke, A. 2007. 'Use of general extenders by German non-native speakers of English'. *International Review of Applied Linguistics in Language Teaching* 45: 141–60.

Terraschke, A. and J. Holmes. 2007. '"Und tralala": Vagueness and general extenders in German and New Zealand English'. In J. Cutting (ed.), *Vague Language Explored.* London: Palgrave. 198–220.

Tognini-Bonelli, E. 1993. 'Interpretative nodes in discourse: *Actual* and *actually*'. In M. Baker, G. Francis and E. Tognini-Bonelli (eds), *Text and Technology: In Honour of John Sinclair.* Amsterdam and Philadelphia: John Benjamins. 193–211.

Traugott, Elizabeth C. and Richard Dasher. 2002. *Regularity in Semantic Change.* Cambridge: Cambridge University Press.

Verschueren, J. 1999. *Understanding Pragmatics.* London: Arnold Publishers.

—2000. 'Notes on the role of metapragmatic awareness in language use'. *Pragmatics* 10(4): 439–56.

Watts, R. 1989. 'Taking the pitcher to the "well": Native speakers' perception of their use of discourse markers in conversation'. *Journal of Pragmatics* 13: 203–37.

Weydt, H. 2006. 'What are particles good for?' In K. Fischer (ed.), *Approaches to Discourse Particles.* Amsterdam: Elsevier. 205–17.

Wichmann A., A.-M. Simon-Vandenbergen, K. Aijmer. 2010. 'How prosody reflects semantic change: A synchronic case study of *of course*'. In K. Davidse, L. Vandelanotte and H. Cuyckens (eds), *Subjectification, Intersubjectification and Grammaticalization* [Topics in English Linguistics]. Berlin: Mouton de Gruyter. 103–54.

Wierzbicka, A. 1976. 'Particles and linguistic relativity'. *International Review of Slavic Linguistics* 1(2–3): 327–67.

Winter, J. and C. Norrby. 2000. 'Set-marking tags "and stuff"'. In J. Henderson (ed.), *Proceedings of the 1999 Conference of the Australian Linguistic Society.*

Author Index

Subject Index